Date Due

The End of Terrorism?

"Leonard Weinberg, one of the most prominent and prolific scholars of terrorism, offers an excellent account of the demise of terrorist groups. This original, well researched and fascinating book is highly accessible and should become a mandatory reading for anyone who is interested in conflicts and terrorism."

Ami Pedahzur, *University of Texas, Austin, USA*

"Leonard Weinberg's thorough analysis significantly advances our understanding of the compelling question of how terrorism ends. The insights are valuable, and the book is well-grounded in empirical research."

Martha Crenshaw, *Stanford University, USA*

This book considers not the beginning or origins of terrorism but how groups that use terrorism end. Terrorism as a tactic is unlikely to disappear; however, virtually all the groups that employed terrorist violence during the 1960s and 1970s have passed from the scene in one way or another. Likewise most of the individuals who embarked on "careers" in terrorism over these same years now engage in other pursuits.

The author argues that al-Qaeda and the various violent Islamist groups it has inspired are, like their predecessors, bound to bring their operations to an end. Rather than discussing the defection or deradicalization of individuals the book aims to analyze how terrorist groups are defeated, or defeat themselves. It examines the historical record, drawing on a large collection of empirical data to analyze in detail the various ends of these violent organizations.

This book provides a unique, empirically informed perspective on the end of terrorism that is a valuable addition to the currently available literature and will be of interest to scholars of terrorism, security studies, and international politics.

Leonard Weinberg is Professor Emeritus at the University of Nevada, USA and a visiting professor at King's College, University of London, UK.

Routledge Studies in Extremism and Democracy

Series Editors: Roger Eatwell, *University of Bath* and
Matthew Goodwin, *University of Nottingham*
Founding Series Editors: Roger Eatwell, *University of Bath*
and Cas Mudde, *University of Antwerp (UFSIA)*

This new series encompasses academic studies within the broad fields of 'extremism' and 'democracy'. These topics have traditionally been considered largely in isolation by academics. A key focus of the series, therefore, is the (inter-)relation between extremism and democracy. Works will seek to answer questions such as to what extent 'extremist' groups pose a major threat to democratic parties, or how democracy can respond to extremism without undermining its own democratic credentials.

The books encompass two strands:

Routledge Studies in Extremism and Democracy includes books with an introductory and broad focus which are aimed at students and teachers. These books will be available in hardback and paperback. Titles include:

Understanding Terrorism in America
From the Klan to al Qaeda
Christopher Hewitt

Fascism and the Extreme Right
Roger Eatwell

Racist Extremism in Central and Eastern Europe
Edited by Cas Mudde

Political Parties and Terrorist Groups (2nd Edition)
Leonard Weinberg, Ami Pedahzur and Arie Perliger

The New Extremism in 21st Century Britain
Edited by Roger Eatwell and Matthew Goodwin

New British Fascism
Rise of the British National Party
Matthew Goodwin

The End of Terrorism?
Leonard Weinberg

Routledge Research in Extremism and Democracy offers a forum for innovative new research intended for a more specialist readership. These books will be in hardback only. Titles include:

The End of Terrorism?

Leonard Weinberg

Routledge
Taylor & Francis Group

LONDON AND NEW YORK

First published 2012
by Routledge
2 Park Square, Milton Park, Abingdon, Oxon OX14 4RN

Simultaneously published in the USA and Canada
by Routledge
711 Third Avenue, New York, NY 10017

Routledge is an imprint of the Taylor & Francis Group, an informa business

© 2012 Leonard Weinberg

British Library Cataloguing in Publication Data
A catalogue record for this book is available from the British Library

Library of Congress Cataloging in Publication Data
Weinberg, Leonard, 1939–
    The end of terrorism?/Leonard Weinberg.
    p. cm.—(Routledge studies in extremism and democracy)
    Includes bibliographical references and index.
    1. Terrorism. 2. Terrorism—Prevention. I. Title.
    HV6431.W4357 2011
    363.325—dc22   2011006140

ISBN: 978–0–415–78117–6 (hbk)
ISBN: 978–0–415–78118–3 (pbk)
ISBN: 978–0–203–80595–4 (ebk)

Typeset in Times New Roman
by Florence Production Ltd, Stoodleigh, Devon

Contents

Illustrations

Figures

Tables

Abbreviations

AN	National Vanguard
ANC	African National Congress
ANM	Arab Nationalist Movement
AQI	al-Qaeda in Iraq
ARVN	Armed Forces of the Republic of Vietnam
ASG	Abu Sayyaf Group
BR	Red Brigades
DC	Christian Democratic Party
ELN	National Liberation Army
EOKA	National Organization of Cypriot Fighters
ERP	People's Revolutionary Army
ETA	Basque Homeland and Liberty
FARC	People's Revolutionary Armed Forces of Colombia
FATA	Federally Administered Tribal Areas
FLN	National Liberation Front
GAP	Partisan Action Group
IEDs	improvised explosive devices
IMRO	Inner Macedonian Revolutionary Organization
IRA	Irish Republican Army
IRB	Irish Republican Brotherhood
IRP	Islamic Republican Party
ISI	inter-service intelligence agency
KKK	Klu Klux Klan
LC	Lotta Continua
LTTE	Liberation Tigers of Tamil Eelam
MILF	Moro Islamic Liberation Front
MIPT	Memorial Institute for the Study of Terrorism
MNF	Multinational Force
MNLF	Moro National Liberation Front
MSI	Italian Social Movement

NAP	Nuclei of Armed Proletariats
NAR	Nuclei of Armed Revolutionaries
NLF	National Liberation Front
OAS	Secret Army Organization
ON	New Order
PCI	Italian Communist Party
PFLP	Popular Front for the Liberation of Palestine
PIJ	Palestinian Islamic Jihad
PIRA	Provisional Irish Republican Army
PKK	Turkish Worker's Party
PL	Front Line
PLC	Palestinian Legislative Council
PLO	Palestinian Liberation Organization
QST	Quetta Shura Taliban
RAF	Red Army Faction
RAHOWA	racial holy war
RUC	Royal Ulster Constabulary
SDS	Students for a Democratic Society
SID	Defense Intelligence Agency
SLA	Southern Lebanese Army
SLA	Symbionese Liberation Army
TNT	Tamil National Tigers
TP	Third Position
TULF	Tamil United Liberation Front
UDA	Ulster Defence Association
UNRWA	UN Relief and Works Agency
UVF	Ulster Defence Force
VC	Viet Cong
VM	Viet Min

1   Introduction

This is a book about how terrorism ends.[1] The subject may seem surprising because these days it is easy to get the impression that terrorism is virtually endless. Almost a decade after the 9/11 attacks on the World Trade Center and the Pentagon a National Intelligence Estimate reported that al-Qaeda had regrouped and was stronger than ever. In the United States, The National Counter Terrorism Center reported that the number of terrorist incidents had increased on a worldwide basis. Observers inform us that al-Qaeda agents are constantly searching for or attempting to construct weapons of mass destruction: biological and nuclear devices are now major worries.

Furthermore, there seems little reason to rely on fear-inducing estimates of what the future may bring. Early in 2010, suicide bombers were exploding themselves with some frequency in Iraq, Afghanistan, and Pakistan. Groups linked to al-Qaeda are now active in Yemen and Somalia, states with very limited capacities to stop their operations. The Western nations are by no means exempt from these developments. According to a recent estimate, at least thirty terrorist plots against the United States have been foiled since 9/11.[2] So-called "lone wolves" prowl the streets or seek to board the airliners of the Western democracies in search of attractive targets.

Advocates of jihad against the United States and the West more generally define the situation as a protracted struggle, a series of stages leading to the triumph of the "House of Islam" eventually on a worldwide basis.[3] The United States will be expelled from the Middle East and Israel will be destroyed (some mention the year 2023 for this event). For the more imaginative among them, the jihad will culminate with the reestablishment of the Caliphate in the Middle East and the breakdown of the whole European-imposed system of independent states.

If there is a consensus on the matter it is that the current surge in terrorist violence will persist well into the twenty-first century, and perhaps beyond. Is there any reason to believe this assessment is wrong? I do not possess a crystal ball, but what I do possess is some understanding of the historical record. What does this record tell us?

The historian of terrorism David Rapoport thinks that modern terrorism may be divided into four relatively distinct waves.[4] The first wave dates from the last third of the nineteenth century and consisted largely of Russian revolutionaries and European anarchists. The latter were advocates of "propaganda by deed" and believed that by assassinating monarchs, presidents, and other eminent figures the "masses" or workers could be transformed into revolutionaries. The ensuing violence would bring down the prevailing order and usher in a new era of peace and harmony.

Rapoport dates the second wave to the post-World War I era and the pursuit of national independence for those parts of the globe ruled by the various European imperial powers. This wave crested in the two decades following World War II with the achievement of independence by such new nations as India, Pakistan, Algeria, Indonesia, Nigeria, Kenya, Vietnam, Cyprus, and Israel. Rapoport associates the third wave with the 1960s, the anti-Vietnam War protests, university student activism, the Sino-Soviet split and, more generally, to the cause of political revolution. In several Latin American countries, e.g., Uruguay, Argentina, and Brazil, a variety of "urban guerrilla" groups were formed in order to topple military or military-bureaucratic regimes with the goal in mind of redressing the continent's vast inequalities between the wealthy and poor. In Western Europe "new left" bands embarked on what in retrospect appears as a quixotic crusade to make revolutions within the region's prosperous democracies. (To be fair the German groups at least claimed to be acting on behalf of the oppressed of the Third World, the Palestinians in particular.)

The fourth wave was set in motion by religious concerns. In the Muslim world, the Iranian Revolution of 1979 and the Soviet Union's decision, made later during the same year, to invade Afghanistan to prop up a pro-communist regime in Kabul spawned a wave of Islamist terrorism that continues, largely unabated, to this day.

Each of the previous three waves lasted for approximately a generation or roughly thirty years before receding. Virtually all of the groups that were responsible for the terrorism during these periods have passed from the scene. How did this happen? If the previous waves dissipated after a few decades, why not the present fourth wave? And to pose another question: How did terrorism end in the past?

In considering these questions we should clarify our terms and make some basic distinctions. In thinking about how or if terrorism ends we should distinguish between 1) terrorism as a tactic; 2) the individuals who use this tactic—terrorists in other words; and 3) terrorist groups— collections of people who engage in terrorism.

In thinking about its tactical meaning the British political scientist Paul Wilkinson distinguishes terrorism from other modes of violence and conflict based on the following attributes:

- It is premeditated and designed to create a climate of fear.
- It is directed at a wider target than the immediate victims.
- It inherently involves attacks on random or symbolic targets, including civilians.
- It is considered by the society in which it occurs as "extra-normal," that is, in the literal sense that it violates the norms regulating disputes, protests and dissent.
- It is used primarily, though not exclusively, to influence the political behavior of governments, communities or specific social groups.[5]

Given this meaning, it is easy to understand why terrorism has become such an attractive tactic for extremist political groups and organizations around the world. Terrorist attacks, including suicide bombings, are relatively inexpensive and usually not all that difficult to accomplish, relative to the amount of time, effort, and energy governments, especially democratic ones, must devote in order to prevent or respond to these attacks. Thanks to the mass media's needs and the Internet's various possibilities via the social media in particular, relatively weak groups with meager resources can appear to audiences of potential followers or adversaries to be far more powerful than they are in reality.[6] Previously obscure causes and equally obscure groups can be brought to the world's attention, frequently favorable attention, through a handful of spectacular and inexpensive terrorist attacks. As a tactic then, I find it hard to imagine a complete end to terrorist violence in the foreseeable future. The costs are low and the potential benefits evidently too high for terrorism to simply go away.

This conclusion does not mean however that terrorism need be employed by the same cast of characters to achieve the same sets of objectives on an indefinite basis. In fact the tactic may remain about the same—terrorists have relied overwhelmingly on the bomb and the gun since the last third of the nineteenth century (even suicide attacks are not without precedents) —but those individuals and groups using the tactic along with the goals they pursue change significantly over time (see p. 2).

For instance, individuals who have embarked on careers as terrorists need not spend the rest of their lives committing or directing acts of violence. "Once a terrorist always a terrorist," is rarely true. Successful suicide bombers are, of course, another matter, but there are an abundance of individuals who participated in terrorist activities in their youth who then pursued other careers or did other things later in their lives. Here are a few prominent examples. In Northern Ireland Gerry Adams, one time a leader of the paramilitary IRA, now leads a peaceful political party, the Sinn Fein. In Italy during the country's "years of lead" (the 1970s) Antonio Negri was a key figure in Worker Autonomy, a group given over to "diffuse terrorism." Currently, after serving a prison sentence, he has resumed his career as a political philosopher at the University of Padua. In the United States, Bernadine Dohrn, once placed on the FBI's Most Wanted list for her activities in the Weathermen, presently teaches law at Northwestern University. Her husband, Bill Ayres, is a professor of social work at the University of Illinois' Chicago campus. Their earlier careers were called to the public's attention during the 2008 presidential election campaign. In Israel, Menachem Begin and Yitzhak Shamir led the terrorist groups Irgun and Lehi (Fighters for the Freedom of Israel) respectively during the 1940s. Both later became their country's prime minister. Begin later shared the Nobel Peace Prize with Yassir Arafat, president of the Palestinian Authority, but earlier leader of Fatah during its terrorist phase (see Chapter 5). What is true for these well-known figures is equally true for many more individuals who over the years have abandoned terrorism for a wide range of nonviolent pursuits.

The political psychologist John Horgan calls attention to pathways out of terrorism.[7] If becoming a terrorist involves a process of "radicalization" leading to affiliation or identification with a group engaging in terrorism, so too individuals may undergo a process of deradicalization leading them away from terrorism. Growing disillusionment with the group and its goals based on the experience of prolonged group membership may lead individuals to seek "exit" or at least some nonviolent role in the same organization. Departure from terrorism is often facilitated by contacts and support from family, friends, and various interpersonal contacts (boyfriends, girlfriends) that remain outside the terrorist group's orbit or control. In recent years governments in Saudi Arabia, Indonesia, Yemen, and Colombia (among others) have developed programs aimed at providing members of terrorist groups ranging in outlook from al-Qaeda to the people's Revolutionary Armed Forces of Colombia (FARC) with paths away from lives of violence to a return to normal lives and peaceful careers. Saudi Arabia in particular has pursued a program of rehabilitation aimed at turning former terrorists into peaceful subjects. Also, as Horgan points out, individuals may abandon terrorism without necessarily becoming deradicalized. Individuals may retain their radical views but become "disengaged." They may desist from engaging in terrorist violence while still in pursuit of these extreme views. Adams, Begin, Shamir, and Arafat, for example, may very well have retained their commitments to a United Ireland, a Greater Israel or, in Arafat's case, the destruction of the same, while abandoning the gun and the bomb for the ballot box and international diplomacy—for tactical reasons. The same logic applies to what are often labeled "terrorist groups." As we will see later in our discussion, groups that have inflicted terrorist violence may retain their identities and most of their political goals while seeking to attain them by other than terrorist means or in addition to terrorist means.

The ends of terrorist groups

Terrorist groups and terrorist campaigns, like the individuals who participate in them, need not go on forever. During the 1960s and 1970s, during terrorism's third wave in other words, Latin America and Western Europe abounded with revolutionary "urban guerrilla" or terrorist organizations. Germany had the Red Army Faction and June 2nd Movement, Italy the Red Brigades and Front Line, France Direct Action, Belgium the Communist Combatant Cells, Greece the Revolutionary November 17 group, to mention the most prominent. None of these groups exist any longer. The cause of Marxist revolution lost its propulsive power as the cold war drew to a close, the countries of Eastern Europe broke free of communist rule, and the authorities improved their ability to cope with the challenges posed by these Marxist-inspired groups. Further, if we consider the fact that modern terrorism dates from the last third of the nineteenth century, we cannot help but observe that none of the Russian revolutionary, anarchist, and nationalist groups that staged terrorist attacks at the end of the nineteenth and beginning of the twentieth centuries, usually against visible symbols of state authority, are with us any more. Where did they go? What happened to them?

At this point we think it helpful to specify what we mean by "terrorist group." As with individual terrorists, so too with the groups to which these individuals belong there need not be anything permanent about the use of terrorism as a tactic. I regard a terrorist group as one that uses terrorist violence either exclusively or in conjunction with other tactics as a means of achieving its political goals. But groups that challenge governments or other sources of authority in society may exist before and after the adoption of terrorism as a tactic. The separatist organization Basque Homeland and Liberty (ETA) existed for more almost a decade (it was founded in 1959) before it launched its first terrorist attacks (in 1968) on the Spanish government. In fact, as Martha Crenshaw notes, terrorism is rarely the first tactic an oppositional group uses in challenging those in authority.[8] During the 1970s, for example, various revolutionary terrorist groups—e.g., the Red Army Faction or the Weathermen—in Europe and America grew out of the anti-Vietnam War peace movement whose initial tactics involved mass protest and acts of largely peaceful civil disobedience.

In a similar way oppositional groups may persist after they have given up terrorism for other means of political expression. For instance, in the United States the racial supremacist Ku Klux Klan staged terrorist attacks for decades in an effort to prevent African-Americans from achieving equality of rights and liberties with white Southerners. The KKK's terrorism failed to prevent the latter, but the organization (really organizations) has persisted into the twenty-first century and retained its commitment to the cause of racial supremacy ("White Power") as well. Klan terrorism has largely been replaced by protest rallies, Internet websites, public access television appearances, and other ways of gaining publicity. The KKK is hardly an isolated case. The case of the Muslim Brotherhood in Egypt and the IRA in Northern Ireland might also be offered as evidence.

How then do radical oppositional groups, whether or not they endure, end their involvement with terrorism? The most obvious answer is *defeat*.[9]

By their nature terrorist groups are usually weak relative to the governments they challenge. In many cases states are willing to tolerate or even turn a blind eye to terrorist groups to the extent they only represent a minor annoyance, comparable to a small criminal gang. Once the terrorism becomes something more, a potentially serious threat to the state and public order more generally, governments will usually reorder their priorities and do what they can to eliminate the group(s) inflicting the violence. For example, in Italy the government came to perceive the Red Brigades (BR) as a serious threat in 1978 after one of its "columns" kidnapped and later assassinated former prime minister Aldo Moro. After the Moro case, the Italian government, otherwise not noted for its efficiency, created a special police unit aimed at defeating the BR. Parliament enacted new "emergency laws" and other measures. And within a few years the BR's career was brought to a conclusion.[10] In Latin America during the 1970s terrorist groups in Uruguay (the Tupamaros) and Argentina (i.e., the Montoneros, People's Revolutionary Armed Forces) crossed a threshold when they, for example, began killing policemen and military officers—often along with members of their families. These acts mounted to a point where they provoked the military in both countries into overthrowing inept civilian governments. Once in power the new military regimes proceeded to eliminate these "urban guerrilla" bands within a short time and without much difficulty. These results were achieved at the price of suspensions of civil liberties often accompanied by the use of torture and other unsavory tactics.

To be more specific, how then is *defeat* achieved? As the above examples suggest government repression is a common outcome. Members and often sympathizers as well are captured or killed until the group is no longer able to function. Brazil, challenged by multiple "urban guerrilla" organizations in the late 1960s and early 1970s, along with the two other Latin American countries mentioned above, had little difficulty in achieving repression once the proverbial "kid gloves" were removed and the national police and military forces were given or gave themselves free rein. In these cases the cure was worse than the disease, at least from the democratic perspective.

A more limited technique for defeating a terrorist group involves the decapitation of its leadership. By killing or capturing its leaders the affected government may render a terrorist group, particularly one organized along authoritarian lines, directionless; its members confused about how or if to proceed. The Japanese government's arrest of Shoko Asahara, the charismatic leader of the terrorist cult Aum Shinrikyo, in 1995 following its poison gas on the Tokyo subway system, appears to have brought that group's terrorist campaign to a conclusion. On the other hand, the arrests by Peruvian and Turkish authorities of the Shining Path and the Turkish Worker's Party's (PKK) leaders blunted their momentum but hardly brought about their complete defeat. We might make a similar observation about Israel's policy involving the "targeted killing" of the leaders of Hamas, Islamic Jihad, and other Palestinian terrorist organizations during the Al-Aqsa Intifada (2000–2004). The jury is still out on the results of drone strikes on Taliban and al-Qaeda targets in Afghanistan and Pakistan's tribal areas. The attacks though do seem at a minimum to have disrupted their operations.

Terrorist groups may also defeat themselves for reasons having to do with the alienation of their constituents or would be constituents. They may incite a backlash. For instance, on November 17, 1997 at Luxor in Egypt's southern desert,

> six young men dressed in black police uniforms and carrying vinyl bags entered the temple precinct shortly before nine in the morning. One of the men shot a guard, and they then all put on red headbands identifying themselves as members of the Islamic Group. Two of the attackers remained at the gate to await the shootout with the

police, who never arrived. The other men crisscrossed the terraced temple grounds, mowing down tourists by shooting their legs, then methodically finishing them off with close shots to the head. They paused to mutilate some of the bodies with butcher knives. One elderly Japanese man was eviscerated . . . The killing went on for forty-five minutes, until the floors streamed with blood. The dead included a five-year old British child and four Japanese couples on their honeymoons. The ornamented walls were splattered with brains and bits of hair.[11]

Egyptians throughout the country were embarrassed and repelled by this act of barbaric violence. The Luxor killings ignited a backlash against the Islamic Group (al-Gama'a al-Islamiyya). The Group, which had previously enjoyed wide support among Egyptian university students in particular, suffered a precipitous decline in popularity. (Even if this decline in support was just a widespread perception it offered the Egyptian police carte blanche in the unrestricted use of force.)

The Egyptian example represents a case in which the very constituency the terrorist group claims to represent turns against it. In other words, the group may defeat itself by setting off a backlash. Other cases could be brought to bear. Following the murder of former Italian Prime Minister Aldo Moro in 1978, for example, the public came to regard Moro as a hero and martyr and his Red Brigades' killers with disdain. The mass media demanded that the government do more to defeat the organization.[12] The decision to kill Moro also set off factional divisions within the Red Brigades, usually a sign that a terrorist group has entered the "endgame" phase of its career.

Another case: In Iraq the al-Qaeda attacks (2005–2006) on Sunnis thought to sympathize with American and Shiite goals were so brutal and often indiscriminate that the tribal leaders became willing to negotiate agreements with the US military to bring an end to al-Qaeda's terrorist attacks in and around Baghdad. Although how long these agreements last presently (2011) remains to be seen.

Terrorist groups may also defeat themselves for essentially internal reasons, what Ross and Gurr describe as "burnout."[13] We should remember that in most cases terrorist groups are voluntary organizations. Why should individuals join or members continue to contribute effort if the group's aims appear increasingly out of reach, or even, if reached, not as worthwhile as originally believed? Why continue to risk your life for a hopeless cause? Why become what the novelist Graham Greene referred to as a "burnout case"?

The Egyptian group al-Jihad decided to desist from violence after its leadership reached the conclusion that terrorism was incompatible with the Koran's principles. Al-Jihad's decision was surprising in view of the facts that it not only carried out the assassination of Egyptian President Sadat in 1981 but one of its early leaders, Dr Ayman al-Zawahiri, became a founder of al-Qaeda. In fact a substantial percentage of al-Qaeda's first generation of recruits was drawn from the Egyptian al-Jihad.[14]

In some instances terrorist group members may reach the conclusion that the goals themselves may no longer be worth pursuing. The end of the cold war, the collapse of the Soviet Union, and China's transformation into a capitalist country helped persuade terrorist group members in the industrialized democracies that Marxism–Leninism or Maoism was not the wave of the future. Why continue to stage terrorist attacks if the very models of "real socialism" had opted for the marketplace and private enterprise? Perhaps a handful of diehards would continue the struggle, at least for a while, but terrorist groups with this left-wing revolutionary bent will in all likelihood have difficulty in recruiting a new generation of members under these circumstances.

Further, Cynthia Irvin reminds us that terrorist groups are likely to be composed of three types of members: ideologues, radicals, and politicos. "Ideologues are often 'hard' men and women . . . They are drawn to action more than political discussion, and they are committed to the belief that organizational goals can only be obtained as a result of the armed struggle of their military wings."[15] Radicals share the ideologues' commitment to action but sense that violence alone will not be sufficient to achieve the group's goals. They support the use of terrorist violence as a tactic not as a means of personal catharsis. Politicos, on the other hand, "are far more willing than their more militarist counterparts to acknowledge that acts of political violence, particularly in which noncombatants are killed, invite both crippling repression and the organization's alienation from all but its core base."[16] Over time these competing perspectives frequently give rise to intra-group tensions and factional divisions. (Governments often have considerable ability to promote these via the use of agents provocateur and other measures.) The history of the Basque nationalist group ETA in Spain with its multiple divisions is illustrative. Over the years factions have broken away to create new groups, some committed to entering the realm of peaceful party politics, others to continuing the armed struggle, while still others stand for some combination of both violence and conventional forms of political expression. Inevitably in such a setting some individual members grow weary of the in-fighting and withdraw to private life.

Democracies often have to pay a price for defeating terrorist groups. The price involves the violation of the democracies' own principles. Rights to privacy, freedom of travel, access to an attorney, speedy trial, or even a trial itself no matter how speedy ("preventive detention," "enemy combatant"), freedom from torture (water-boarding), and other unusual punishments have all been jeopardized by the responses of democratic governments to terrorist threats both domestic and international. Authoritarian regimes rarely suffer from these constitutional restraints. Illustratively, following the Ayatollah Khomeini's ascendancy in Iran after the Shah was forced into exile (1979–1980), the new Islamic Republic was confronted by a serious terrorist threat (1981). Groups of secular-minded, anti-Khomeini Mujaheddin and Fedayeen launched a series of devastating terrorist attacks, including the killing of the country's newly elected president and the bombing of the headquarters of the Islamic Republican Party, an attack that killed many leading figures in the new clerical regime. Revolutionary Guards and other followers of Khomeini responded to the challenge with great brutality. They tortured and killed captured Mujaheddin and Fedayeen without regard to humanitarian principles to the point of dragging wounded terrorist suspects out of hospitals and denying them treatment. The result was a rapid end to terrorist activity in Iran.[17]

Oppositional groups may also end their use of terrorism because they have achieved *success*. This is a very rare outcome, as we shall see. If we measure the success of terrorist tactics based on the ultimate aims the groups involved say they intend to achieve, the results suggest few successes. Max Abrahams examined the performances of twenty-eight groups identified as terrorist groups by the US State Department in 2001. He found only a handful had reached their self-defined objectives five years later.[18] *Success* is a rarity but it does occur. In the period of worldwide decolonization following the end of World War II a few terrorist groups got what they wanted. On Cyprus, the British would probably not have withdrawn so quickly if it had not been for Colonel George Grivas and his EOKA organization. About the same may be said of the role of Menachem Begin's Irgun in the British mandate of Palestine and that of the National Liberation Front in driving the French from Algeria. In these cases and perhaps a handful of others, *success* was achieved because the groups involved employed a variety of tactics in addition to terrorist violence and enjoyed the external support of national states and groups sympathetic to their causes.

In addition to members, terrorist groups like other voluntary organizations need money and supplies in order to survive. Often meeting these needs has involved state sponsorship. Some states in South Asia, the

Middle East, and North Africa have found it advantageous to fund terrorist groups willing to stage attacks on the state sponsors' enemies. The benefit is that the states involved can distance themselves from the attacks by denying involvement out of fear of the consequences of committing an act of war. For example, during the 1990s Pakistan funded and provided arms for such Kashmiri groups as Jaish-e-Mohammad and Lashkar-e-Tayyeba seeking the cessation of that Indian state with a heavily Muslim population and either its national independence or its merger with Pakistan.[19] The rulers in Islamabad were aware that a direct military confrontation with India over Kashmir would likely prove disastrous—as it had in the past. The use of pawns or proxies has its advantages. But over time states often find the state sponsorship of terrorist groups has its drawbacks. Target states challenged by state-sponsored terrorist groups may respond by applying economic sanctions and threatening or using military force directly against the sponsor. Condemnation by the United Nations and other international organizations may help as well. Libya under the leadership of Colonel Qaddafi was persuaded to turn away from its support of the Abu Nidal organization and other terrorist groups as a result of the application of these sanctions.

If states fail to offer support where do terrorist groups turn? One answer is philanthropy. Wealthy sympathizers may be willing to supply the needed support. Al-Qaeda, for instance, has long been the beneficiary of contributions by wealthy patrons in Saudi Arabia and various oil-rich Persian Gulf sheikdoms. Following 9/11, however, the Saudi and other governments involved have come under intense pressure from the United States to block the transfer of money from local patrons to foreign terrorists.

If external funding and support becomes unavailable, where do terrorist groups turn? The answer in many instances has been criminal activity. Bank robbery, the kidnapping for ransom of wealthy or well-connected individuals, murder for hire, and drug trafficking have all become effective means by which terrorist groups are able to sustain themselves. The problem with criminal activity is that it may prove too effective.

Terrorist groups that began with a clear political agenda may transform themselves into straightforward criminal bands more interested in the acquisition of wealth than advancing the cause. This tendency becomes pronounced when the members' backgrounds include criminal activity. (In Western Europe and North America it was not uncommon for terrorists to have been recruited while serving prison terms for nonpolitical offenses). The history of modern terrorism provides any number of examples, from the Inner Macedonian Revolutionary Organization (IMRO) in the early twentieth century to components of the Palestinian Liberation Organization during the 1980s to elements within the Irish Republican Army (IRA) at the beginning of the twenty-first century.

This criminalization of an essentially political group calls to mind another way in which terrorist groups end their careers. They may *transform* themselves into peaceful participants in the country's political process or they may also *transform* themselves into a full-fledged insurrectionary armed force. For example, during the apartheid era in South Africa Nelson Mandela's African National Congress (ANC) developed a terrorist organization, the Spear of the Nation, to carry out small-scale terrorist attacks against symbols of white supremacy. When Mandela was released from prison and an end to apartheid was achieved through negotiations, the Spear of the Nation simply became part of the ANC, the winning party at all subsequent South African elections. Another case: in Uruguay the Tupamaros were repressed by the country's military in 1972. When the military finally permitted the restoration of democracy in 1983, the Tupamaros reappeared, this time as a peaceful political party running candidates for public office.[20] The IRA in Northern Ireland offers an outstanding case of *transformation*. Following the "Good Friday" agreement of 1998 the organization went through a transformation from a paramilitary group staging attacks in London, Birmingham, and on the streets of Belfast, into a political party the Sinn Fein (previously its political wing) participating in provincial and parliamentary elections and serving in the government of Northern Ireland.[21]

Terrorist violence may also lead not to peace but to internal war. During the era of decolonization, the 1950s and 1960s, some of the writing about terrorism defined it as part of the early "agitation-propaganda" phase of a long-term insurgency. The insurgents used terrorism, e.g., the assassination of local government representatives in the villages, detonating bombs at public places in the cities, murdering political rivals and members of the colonial power, to capture the public's attention.[22] Once this task is accomplished the insurgents escalate their struggle into a full-fledged guerrilla war against the incumbent regime. Walter Laqueur reports the following account of Bernard Fall's return to South Vietnam:

> Bernard Fall relates that he returned to Vietnam in 1957 after the war [against French rule] had been over for two years and was told by everyone that the situation was fine. He was bothered, however, by the many obituaries in the press of village chiefs who had been

killed by "unknown elements" and "bandits." Upon investigation he found that these attacks were clustered in certain areas and that there was a purpose behind them.[23]

The Viet Cong was announcing its presence.

In reality the Viet Cong not only employed terrorism during the early stages of its campaign against the anti-communist regime in Saigon but throughout its war against the South Vietnamese government and against the American presence. The 1968 TET offensive is illustrative. The simultaneous use of terrorism, guerrilla warfare tactics, and political agitation seems to be characteristic of many contemporary insurgencies. In Sri Lanka for example, the Liberation Tigers of Tamil Eelam (now defeated) was able to transform its terrorist campaign against the Sinhalese-dominated government in Colombo into a full-scale civil war involving conventional battles between the two sides' armed forces— all the while continuing the use of terrorism. The recent fighting in Iraq bears some resemblance. Both Sunni and Shiite contestants for power have used terrorist bombings and such guerrilla warfare tactics as "improvised explosive devices" (IEDs) against American patrols (the Viet Cong used "bunji sticks") along with staging set-piece battles in their efforts to compel the United States to withdraw. In short, terrorist groups may become sufficiently popular to transform their struggles into full-blown insurgencies involving a continuation of terrorism, along with guerrilla war and even conventional warfare.

What follows

This book is about how terrorist groups end. In this introduction I have identified three ways in which these groups end their careers: *defeat*, *success*, and *transformation*. I should alert readers to the fact that these categories need not be mutually exclusive. Imminent *defeat*, for example, may lead to a group's *transformation* into a political party contestant for power in a democratic setting. In Northern Ireland the IRA leadership came to the conclusion that further paramilitary operations in Belfast and elsewhere were unlikely to bring about Irish unification along the lines it favored. The leadership's conclusion leads in turn to the IRA's decision to enter into peace negotiations and the eventual end of terrorism. Other cases could be brought to bear. I think it should suffice to say that these general categories represent central tendencies involving how terrorist groups abandoned the tactic and either disappeared, picked up other tactics or transformed themselves into other forms of political organization.

I have divided most of *The End of Terrorism?* in the following ways. I devote Chapter 2 largely to the work of others: what recent work discloses about the end(s) of terrorist groups, a selective literature review in other words. Further, it is at this point I introduce some findings based on data collected by the National Security Center at the University of Haifa in Israel. Aside from a few details about its collection, I provide a frequency distribution identifying the most common ways in which terrorism ends. In Chapter 3, I focus on the defeat of terrorist groups. What best explains their defeat? I pay particular attention to how or if democracies have been able to bring about this result. Are authoritarian regimes, in the absence of the rule of law and other safeguards, better at inflicting defeat on challenger groups who use terrorist tactics? In Chapter 4, I review cases of *success*, instances in which the use of terrorism in conjunction with other tactics has proved successful in achieving the challenging group's goals. How common have been the successes and under what circumstances have these successes been achieved? I devote Chapter 5 to the *transformation* of terrorist groups. My focus shifts to groups that retained their organizational forms but shifted their goals (from politics to crime) as well as to groups that underwent an organizational change while maintaining, more or less, their aims. How and under what conditions do they become peaceful political actors abandoning the bomb and the gun in favor of the speaking platform and the ballot box? Or, what accounts for the replacement of political objectives into largely criminal ones? In Chapter 6, I make use of the findings to engage in what I hope will be informed speculation about how al-Qaeda and other contemporary terrorist groups are likely to end their careers in violence.

2 The ends of the affair

In thinking about how terrorist groups end their careers, with a bang or whimper, we ought to pay attention to what some other observers have had to say about this subject. After all we are hardly writing on a completely blank slate. Much of the writing on the subject has been focused on individual cases rather than terrorist groups taken in the aggregate. How did the Liberation Tigers of Tamil Eelam end its campaign of separatist violence against the Sri Lankan government? How and why did the Irish Republican Army turn away from terrorism? Whatever happened to those "urban guerrilla" groups active in much of Latin America that hoped to spark a revolution during the 1970s? At about the same time Germans, Italians, and Japanese were worried that the Red Army Faction, Red Brigades, and United Japanese Red Army would cause major disruptions to their democratic societies. As it turned out, however, these groups didn't amount to all that much. Aside from a few eccentrics here and there, none of them exist any longer. What brought about their collapse: Defections? Repression? The zeitgeist?

These questions have been answered by a variety of case studies. We intend to begin the analysis by reporting what some of these studies tell us about the ends of different groups—suggestive ways by which terrorist bands meet or have met their ends. The benefits of these studies seem obvious. They provide us with detailed accounts of how particular terrorist groups in particular settings ended. Yet these exemplary accounts leave us with an important problem. We still do not know how representative these cases are of terrorist groups in general. Of course some would argue that generalizing about terrorist groups is a virtual impossibility. Given the wide variety of goals, sizes, membership characteristics, and methods of operation that terrorist groups have displayed over the decades, generalizing about them is a fruitless exercise.[1] What, after all, does al-Qaeda in Iraq (AQI) have in common with the Symbionese Liberation Army, the Liberation Tigers of Tamil Eelam, or Robin Hood and his Merry Men, for that matter?

What is true in this instance is true of the social sciences in general. By moving from the specific case to the general observers lose details but derive benefit from understanding what is usually true about the subject under investigation. So in addition to providing a summary of how several violent groups ended their careers in terrorism, I intend to report the work of two general studies of how such groups ended their operations. Finally, I want to introduce readers to the results of an inquiry based on a data set compiled by the national security studies center at the University of Haifa. How do these results compare with those of the other general studies? If they are similar, we ought to have added confidence in the findings. We will have a better sense of how terrorist groups end in a general sense.

Case studies

Some terrorist groups are quite ephemeral, lasting no more than a few months. One analyst, David Rapoport, estimates that the average duration of terrorist groups is no more than one year.[2] For instance, during the height of Italy's terrorist crisis in the 1970s small groups of young people seeking to emulate the major revolutionary bands active in the country would often give themselves an important-sounding label, carry out a few terrorist attacks (e.g., Molotov cocktails thrown at police stations and American consulates, rough up other students and teachers whom they identified as "fascist") and then, bored, move on to some other ways of amusing themselves. At about the same time Great Britain was the site of the Angry Brigade—observers could never quite determine what its members were angry at—that set off bombs here and there (postal boxes were favorite targets) before disappearing from view. Approximately the same may be said in regard to the activities of the Red Youth in the Netherlands. Such groups typically did not do enough damage or last long enough to warrant inclusion in the various terrorism data sets or to justify full-blown treatments as case studies; nor should they. Such groups usually end their operations as the result of their members' ennui rather than dramatic interventions from the outside, and are more a fad than anything else. In this first section of the chapter I will confine the analysis to groups of some consequence.

The Montoneros

Latin America during the 1960s, 1970s, and beyond abounded with "urban guerrilla" organizations committed to the revolutionary overthrow of incumbent regimes from Colombia and Venezuela in the north to

Argentina in the south. The context for their emergence reflected both theory and practice. For many of the young Latinos and Latinas who participated in these groups Che Guevara served as both an inspiration and warning. Che's attempt to apply the lessons of Castro's revolution (1959) in Cuba had met with disaster in the Andes. Bolivian authorities had tracked down and killed Che at his base of operations in the high mountains without all that much difficulty. Yet Fidel Castro had warned that "cities were the graveyards of revolution." This was also a time when the theories of Mao Tse-tung were widely admired throughout the region. Che, a charismatic figure if ever there was one, equipped with what seemed like a winning revolutionary formula, had been defeated. Theories that stressed the role of rural foci in exciting revolutionary fervor among the peasants had not worked. What went wrong?

For such revolutionary Latin American writers as Carlos Marighella (Brazil) and Abraham Guillen (Uruguay), the answer was to be found in terrorism or "urban guerrilla" activity.[3] They reasoned that Latin American cities should become the centers of revolutionary violence. Increasingly the continent's vast urban conurbations—Buenos Aires, Rio de Janeiro, Sao Paulo, Bogota, Montevideo, and Lima—were the locations where revolutions could be centered. The countryside, they reasoned, was losing its centrality in the struggle because its population was declining as millions of peasants moved to the cities in pursuit of better lives. Accordingly Latin America's major metropolitan areas typically contained enormous shanty towns or *barrios* and *favelas* whose impoverished residents, often recent arrivals from the countryside, could be transformed into revolutionaries by the exemplary actions of a vanguard; urban guerrillas in other words.

The cities had certain advantages. The military or bureaucratic-authoritarian regimes that controlled the country were headquartered in the cities. Their instruments of control, e.g., ministries of the interior, police officers, offered tempting targets. The cities were also home to the mass media. They might ignore attacks carried out in the countryside, but they would provide invaluable publicity if terrorist bombings, bank robberies, and kidnappings could be carried out in the major cities. Furthermore, the urban guerrillas could hide in the shanty towns that were often "no go" areas for the police and military. And if the latter decided to stage large-scale raids in these shanty towns in order to capture the guerrillas they might very well so antagonize the local residents that they became sympathetic to the revolutionary cause. So, at least, was the theory of the urban guerrilla.

The situation in Argentina appeared so dreadful that at least for a while it seemed as if these theories might actually bear some relationship to reality. Despite its status as a relatively advanced country with modern economic and government institutions, Argentina had not developed a stable democracy by the time the Montoneros emerged from various student groups in the 1960s. Military juntas and nominal civilian regimes had oscillated in power since the former ousted Juan Peron from power in 1955. Peron, a military officer himself, had ruled the country from 1943 until he was forced into exile following the coup.

Peron along with his first wife Eva had exerted enormous influence on Argentine life during his period in power. In particular he had won the hearts of the "shirtless ones," the country's working class and its union organizations. Following his ouster:

> The military coup ushered in nearly twenty years of political chaos, during which neither military nor civilian governments were able to reconcile the social forces set in motion during the Peron years. The shadow of Peronism loomed over all of the nation's institutions. The series of post-Peron governments tried nearly everything— reconciliation, repression, cooptation, and cooperation—in a host of strategies for effective rule, but they all had the same result, failure.[4]

It was in this context that the Montoneros, along with other urban guerrilla groups, appeared in 1968. The Montoneros' origins were relatively unusual. Unlike its principal competitor the Trotskyite People's Revolutionary Army (ERP) the group was not steeped in the ideology of Marxism–Leninism. Nor did it represent a rebellion against Argentina's or Latin America's numerous and increasingly bureaucratic communist parties. It was not part of what Regis Debray described as "the revolution within the revolution." Instead, the Montoneros emerged as part of an expression of Catholic activism.[5] Its founders drew their inspiration from Pope Paul's 1967 proclamation *Populorum progressio* that condemned economic inequality, the profit motive, racism, and the greed of rich nations in the face of worldwide poverty. These and other statements by Latin American bishops, linked to Vatican II, provided a rationale for the Montoneros' quest for social justice through urban guerrilla operations.

The Monteneros went through a two-year period of preparation (not unlike similar groups in other countries) before launching their campaign of violence in 1970. Who did they attack and why? Richard Gillespie suggests the label "terrorist" is a misnomer because the organization, especially at its beginning, did not stage indiscriminate attacks on civilian targets. Rather it tended to attack outposts and symbols of government authority in the manner of rural guerrillas in various Third World countries.[6] Yet in addition to these targets the Montoneros engaged in a wave of kidnappings—foreign businessmen were favorite targets—bank robberies, and attacks on civilians its leaders regarded as defenders of military rule. Most spectacularly in May 1970 the organization managed to kidnap and then assassinate Pedro Aramburo, a former president of Argentina condemned because of his ties to the military.

The answer to the "why" question is that the Montoneros' leadership hoped to achieve social justice through the return to power of Juan Peron, the perceived champion of the Argentine working class. Peron's views, to the extent he was willing to disclose them, represented an amalgam of ardent nationalism (meaning anti-Americanism along with some muted manifestations of anti-Semitism) and some version of socialism. He was hardly above the use of violence in the pursuit of his goals.[7] Some observers have attached the label "fascist" to his practices; whether the label fits remains to be seen.[8] Peron though was certainly an admirer of Mussolini and spent most of his exile living comfortably in Franco's Spain. Also, we should not forget that various Nazi war criminals, including Adolph Eichmann, Dr Joseph Mengele, and Ante' Pavelic, the head of the Croat fascist group Ustacha, found safe haven in Argentina during Peron's first period of rule (1943–1955).

In the early 1970s the Montoneros were able to recruit new members from the Peronist Youth in order to wage their terrorist and urban guerrilla campaign against the military-backed government in Buenos Aires.[9] Their goal was a return of Peron to power. And from his Madrid exile Peron endorsed their violence.

Argentina's military leadership began to see the writing on the wall and permitted the restoration of democratic elections. The latter were held in March 1973 and the voters chose Hector Campora, from the Peronist Justicialist Liberation Front, as the country's new president. Crowds in Buenos Aires and elsewhere in the country were jubilant. The following year when Peron returned from his exile and was himself elected president, after Campora stepped or was pushed aside, they were beside themselves. The Montoneros not only declared a truce but participated in the jubilation. For the occasion, they declared: "Today, Peron is Argentina. He is Sovereignty. He is Fatherland!"[10] Not only did the Montoneros declare an end to their violence but participated, along with other Peronist youth groups, in the president's parliamentary coalition.

The jubilation and the nonviolence did not last long. As it turned out Peron had used or "instrumentalized" the Montoneros as a means of returning to power. He had little need for them once he had resumed the presidency. Within a short time Peron began condemning the Montoneros' revolutionary goals and expressions of admiration for Che

Guevara. Peron was there to promote modest reformist policies not transform Argentina into a new Cuba. Montonero disenchantment followed as did a resumption of urban guerrilla operations.

Peron, a man in his late seventies, died at the beginning of July 1974. He was then succeeded by his wife Isabel, Argentina's vice-president. A former professional dancer with virtually no political experience, Isabel Peron became the leader of a country with manifold economic and political problems, problems it quickly became apparent she had little capacity to solve. The Montoneros, the ERP, and various other revolutionary groups rapidly escalated their violent attacks to a level higher than they had been before Peron's return to power. Not only did the new wave of violence intensify but it also became more indiscriminate with the groups staging attacks on the families of police and military officers. The situation verged on the chaotic.

Violence and terrorism in Argentina were by no means a monopoly of would-be revolutionaries. In these years the Triple A, the Argentine Anti-Communist Alliance, consisting largely of right-wing "death squads," played a vigilante role in society. They drew up hit lists of priests, journalists, students, and teachers they believed were involved in revolutionary activities or harbored revolutionary sympathies. Oftentimes the lists were published in the press. Those on them were warned to leave the country or suffer the consequences. A few did but most of those named did not. These individuals then became the targets for abduction and assassination.

By 1976 Argentina's military had had enough, as had a significant segment of the public. Isabel Peron was deposed while a patient in hospital, and a junta consisting of Army, Navy, and Air Force chiefs assumed responsibility for running the country. What followed was the so-called "dirty war" during which the military engaged in wholesale and extra-legal detentions of people suspected of belonging to or even sympathizing with the revolutionary groups, including the Montoneros.[11] Thousands were rounded up in this way, oftentimes suspects were taken off the streets by agents in mufti and dragged into unmarked cars and then driven to such places as the Navy Mechanics School. There they were tortured into disclosing whatever information the torturers thought they possessed. After this experience the "disappeared ones" were typically killed, sometimes by being dropped from helicopters into the Atlantic.

This purge of Argentine society lasted for several years. Close to ten thousand people were killed. The Montoneros were not only defeated but largely annihilated, along with the other revolutionary groups. In a sense the Montoneros and the others were victims of their own success.

They succeeded in disrupting Argentine society to such an extent that their presence became intolerable to the military and to major sections of the country's citizens who cheered enthusiastically as tanks rolled through the streets of Buenos Aires.

Algeria and the National Liberation Front (FLN)

Events in Algeria between the launching of the National Liberation Front's revolutionary insurgency in 1954 and the attainment of national independence in 1962 had far-reaching ramifications. As a result of this struggle France underwent a regime change, from the Fourth to an executive dominated Fifth Republic. The principal insurgent group, the National Liberation Front (FLN), became a model for other insurrectionary organizations, most notably the Palestinian Liberation Organization (PLO).

The setting: Algeria had been in France's possession since the middle of the nineteenth century. By the time the full-blown insurrection broke out in 1954 Algeria was treated as an administrative unit, including three *departments*, of metropolitan France. Voters, almost all Europeans, were able to elect representatives to the Chamber of Deputies in Paris. Unlike its other colonies in North Africa and elsewhere, the French regarded Algeria as a part of France. The reason for this treatment had to do with the composition of Algeria's population. Unlike its other colonies, Algeria had a very substantial population, over one million, of European settlers. It was they who were regarded as French citizens and consequently enjoyed the right to vote. The vast majority of the population consisted of Arab and Berber Muslims who possessed, with a handful of exceptions, no such rights.

Violent antagonism between the indigenous Algerians and the European settlers did not begin in 1954. In May 1945 the town of Setif, not far from Constantine, was the site of a slaughter. Following a VE Day parade, young Muslims, apparently egged on by women expressing their pleasure by making loud ululations, went on a rampage through the town killing Europeans, including women and children, as they made their way. Predictably enough the French authorities carried out a series of reprisals in which many Algerians were killed, also on an indiscriminate basis.[12] To say the two populations were polarized would be something of an understatement.

It was against this background of mutual suspicion and hostility that the FLN launched its war for Algerian independence. The FLN's initial tactics involved a rural-based guerrilla insurgency including sealing the country's border with Tunisia to prevent the infiltration of fighters and supplies. The French military's effort, strongly influenced by its recent experiences in Indo-China, was largely successful. Guerrilla tactics did not work in terrain that bore little resemblance to the rainforests of Southeast Asia. The FLN leadership though was not to be deterred by this setback.[13] In August 1955 it promoted a mass uprising in the city of Constantine. The uprising, according to Martha Crenshaw, strongly resembled the 1945 killings in Setif in that Europeans of all circumstances—men, women and children—were killed on an indiscriminate basis. In reaction the European settlers staged protests that included indiscriminate attacks on Algerians in retaliation. And, as with Setif, French military forces launched a brutal crackdown.

The settlers, especially the wealthy landowners—the *colons*—demanded that the government in Paris take more vigorous and consistent action to protect them from these attacks. The Socialist government of Premier Guy Mollet responded by replacing a liberal-minded governor general with an individual, Robert Lacoste, with a clear-cut commitment to retaining a French Algeria. The government also made a commensurate commitment to raising troop levels towards this goal.

1956 was the year in which the fighting escalated substantially. The FLN waged its "Battle of Algiers." This highly publicized campaign was provoked by Lacoste's decision to guillotine condemned Algerian prisoners and an indiscriminate bombing of an apartment building (apparently carried out by ultra-right-wing settlers) in which scores of Algerians were killed. In response the FLN leadership launched or relaunched a campaign of urban terrorism in Algiers. Bombings and other types of terrorist attacks were carried out on an indiscriminate basis against places where European settlers congregated. Places where European young people met were especially attractive targets. Under these circumstances the settlers' feelings of hatred towards the Algerians became incandescent and the *pied noirs* (French settlers) responded with their own terrorist attacks on Muslims who happened to be in the wrong place at the wrong time.

In a spiral of attack and counter-attack, the FLN responded by employing what was originally a French worker tactic, the general strike.[14] By economic standards, the strike was not a victory, but it did achieve a theatrical success. Its audience included the United Nations' General Assembly, which put the Algerian question on its agenda.

The level of antagonism between the French military in Algeria, the settler community, and the government of the Fourth Republic in Paris escalated substantially. The generals and the *colons* accused the already shaky government of not doing enough to support the retention of a

French Algeria. In 1958 these defenders of *Algérie Française* threatened insurrection. They organized "Committees of Public Safety" not only in Algeria but also on Corsica and a few places in metropolitan France. They demanded a savior to rescue the country during its moment of peril. The heroic figure they had in mind was Charles de Gaulle, the leader of the Free French during World War II.

De Gaulle had been living in retirement in a small town not far from Paris. With the consent of the French parliament and the government de Gaulle was brought back to power. He was granted emergency powers and the ability to rule by decree for a period of six months. During this period he toured Algeria and delivered speeches to cheering crowds of Europeans in Algiers, Oran, and Constantine. The crowds cheered what they thought they had heard, namely de Gaulle's commitment to a French Algeria. Yet this was not his intention at all.

As the right-wing politician Jean-Louis Tixier-Vignancour remarked at the time, "if there was an Olympic event for ingratitude, de Gaulle would win the Gold Medal." Because within a short time after his tour of Algeria he announced his intention to open negotiations with the FLN leadership. He had been brought to power largely by the defenders of the *Algérie Française*. Now he had betrayed their cause.

De Gaulle broke the Gordian knot of the stalemated French system.[15] He had a new constitution written, the Fifth Republic's, and approved by the voters. The latter substantially raised the powers of the French president, particularly in foreign affairs, and lowered those of the parliament. It was in this context that de Gaulle sought to end France's entanglement with Algeria.

While negotiations were under way with the FLN violence did not subside in Algeria itself, far from it. In the years between de Gaulle's assumption of the presidency in 1959 and the 1962 Evian agreement that called for Algerian independence, terrorism mounted. FLN units continued to launch attacks against European civilians. The FLN slogan, either the suitcase or the coffin (displayed as graffiti on walls in Algiers and elsewhere) provided the settlers with a stark choice: either leave or die.

Some *pied noirs* refused to accept these were their only options. Along with a collection of rebellious army officers they formed the Secret Army Organization (OAS) to retain French control of Algeria. With this aim in mind the OAS launched its own campaign of terrorism. Their revenge-seeking agents not only set off bombs intended to kill as many Algerians as possible on an indiscriminate basis, intended to make further peace negotiations impossible, but they also carried out attacks in France itself. These included multiple assassination attempts against President de Gaulle himself—at least one of which almost succeeded.

Adding to the extreme volatility of the situation was a military rebellion in Algeria. Parachute units commanded by General Raul Salan threatened to invade the mainland. At one point de Gaulle went on French television and appealed to citizens to go to Orly airport and stand on the tarmac in order to prevent transport planes carrying the paratroopers from landing and seizing control of the government.

The planes never arrived and the rebellion fizzled, after de Gaulle was assured the support of most French military leaders. The Evian agreement providing for Algerian independence was signed in 1962 and overwhelmingly approved at a referendum by French voters.

Was the FLN's terrorist campaign a success? In responding to this question in the affirmative there is some danger of committing the logical fallacy of *post hoc ergo proper hoc*: The belief that because something happens before something else occurred the former *caused* the latter. As we all know, however, the fact that someone performed a rain dance before a cheering crowd in a drought-stricken community does not mean that the dancer caused an ensuing rainstorm despite winning the crowd's admiration for the performance.

FLN terrorism seems to have been more a theatrical success than a military one. In 1957 French forces under the leadership of General Jacque Massu achieved a major success in their confrontation with the FLN in Algiers. Alistair Horne writes:

> No one could doubt the paras [elite parachute units] had scored a major victory for the French Army. They had faced up to a major confrontation with the FLN and won hands down . . . For the FLN the immediate consequence was to force it to face up to a serious defeat and completely review its strategy. Henceforth, it realized that large-scale terrorism in the cities would have to be abandoned. Thus it would conclude the war could no longer really be won inside Algeria itself.[16]

The terrorism certainly helped but the FLN was able to achieve its strategic aims because of the involvement of other factors. At the international level we are dealing with a period of decolonization and of national independence movements, where, in other words, the winds of change were blowing against a continued French presence in North Africa. In France and elsewhere the mass media called attention to torture inflicted by the French forces against hapless Muslim civilians. Public opinion showed declining support for a seemingly unending and expensive commitment to the maintenance of French control of Algeria —on behalf of a relatively small population of European settlers. These factors along with disruptive terrorist activities accelerated France's decision to permit Algerian independence.

Northern Ireland and the IRA

So far in the analysis we have considered a case in which the use of terrorism proved a disaster from the point of view of its perpetrators (the Montoneros) and one in which the FLN achieved its strategic goals, an independent Algeria, though in this case the violence in and of itself was not sufficient to cause the French to end their occupation. In Northern Ireland we now come to a case where negotiations worked and where the IRA achieved some of its aims, in return for which it abandoned the gun and the bomb for the ballot box.

With the likely exception of the Israeli–Arab conflict and perhaps al-Qaeda's recent operations, more has been written in English about the struggle over Northern Ireland than any subject relating to terrorism. Despite the enormous body of commentary, the situation in general may be summarized briefly.

Ireland had been part of the United Kingdom for centuries before members of the Irish Republican Brotherhood (IRB) and others launched an insurgency to win national independence in the years following World War I. Efforts to achieve Home Rule through popular agitation and parliamentary representation had not achieved this intermediate objective. Among other things the province's Protestant population resisted vigorously. Its spokesmen expressed serious fear of being dominated by Ireland's large Catholic majority. Protestant militias in Ulster (Belfast and the northern six counties) were prepared to fight to prevent this eventuality. Nevertheless, by the outbreak of World War I in 1914 the government in London had promised Home Rule. It failed to make good on this promise though; because of the war Britain failed to fulfill its agreement with the Irish leadership.[17] During the war members of the IRB staged the "Easter Rising" in April 1916. They seized control of the post office and other public buildings in Dublin. The British reacted with considerable brutality. British Prime Minister David Lloyd George sent regular army units to repress the uprising. Executions by the British of the uprising's leaders transformed them into martyrs.

Following the end of World War I the struggle for a free Ireland resumed. The fighting between the IRA, which had emerged in the wake of the "Easter Rising," and British forces, the "Black and Tans," resulted in the 1920 Government of Ireland Act. This legislation provided for the division of the island into a "Free State," whose capital was Dublin, and a Northern Ireland provincial government in Belfast to administer Ulster or the six counties on behalf of London. The Protestant majority in Ulster was mollified but substantial elements among the "republican" population in the south were not. They wanted a united and independent Ireland completely free of British control. The IRA became the champion of this cause.[18]

This brief account serves as the background for "The Troubles" that erupted in Northern Ireland in the second half of the 1960s. The proximate cause for the renewed conflict was the status of the province's Catholic minority. This minority was the victim of various forms of discrimination in housing, employment, and voting: the constituencies were arranged in such a way as to under-represent Ulster's Catholic voters.

We should also recall that the 1960s was the era of civil rights protest in the United States. In the American South and elsewhere the followers of Dr Martin Luther King employed nonviolent civil disobedience to challenge prevailing laws based on racial discrimination. These tactics resonated in Northern Ireland. In August 1968, with the protesters singing "We Shall Overcome," civil rights advocates staged a march through Derry, the province's second city. The government sought to stop the march. Also, Protestant defenders of the status quo ("Orangemen") staged a counter-demonstration. One march followed another. Orange societies celebrating the 1688 victory of the Protestant monarchy over Catholics marched through largely Catholic neighborhoods. Civil rights proponents marched through Protestant areas. The result was an outbreak of violence as rocks, bricks, bottles, and curses flew. "The Troubles" had begun.[19]

It was at this point (1969–1970) that the "paramilitary" groups came into play. The provincial government clearly sided with Ulster's Protestants. It sent the largely Protestant police the Royal Ulster Constabulary (RUC), including the so-called "B Specials" (an officially recognized Protestant militia) into Catholic areas of Belfast and Derry to quell increasingly violent protests. The IRA, on the other side, saw an opportunity to pursue its long-standing demand for a United Ireland. At this point though the organization became divided; there were those with a strong commitment to a Marxist–Leninist agenda who believed an armed struggle was premature. The Provisionals, the other faction, were advocates of armed opposition to the provincial government and continued British control.

The Provisional IRA split away and launched a campaign of violence against the forces of order. Weapons were supplied by well-wishers in various countries including the United States. Libya made donations as well. The Provisionals (PIRA) carried out bank robberies and other criminal acts (forced kickbacks from small businesses) intended to raise money for their campaign. They used violence to defend the Catholic population from Ulster police assaults, especially from the "B Specials." The PIRA attacked civilian targets as well. By 1970 an atmosphere of turmoil prevailed, as "volunteer" Protestant groups began to stage indiscriminate attacks in largely Catholic areas. Public order was on the verge of breakdown. It was then that the Labour government of Prime Minister Harold Wilson decided to send the British army to restore order and protect the Catholic population from further Unionist depredations.

Initially the army's deployment was met with widespread approval among the Ulster population. Within a few months, however, the sentiment soured. Spokesmen for PIRA defined the military presence in anti-colonial terms as an army of occupation. PIRA represented "armed struggle" against these occupiers as part of the long-term war to free all of Ireland from the Crown. Army patrols through the streets of Belfast and Derry were often met with bricks, bottles, and curses coming from groups of Catholic youth. Also, PIRA raised the level of tension still higher by detonating bombs in areas where Protestants congregated.

In response to these developments the British imposed a policy of internment without trial. Suspected PIRA members were swept off the streets and interned (jailed) without benefit of *habeas corpus*. These sweeps led to further mass protests. The result was "Bloody Sunday," January 30, 1972. In Derry a crowd protesting "internment" was met by the Army, paratroopers in armored personnel carriers and carrying loaded rifles. The paratroopers fired their weapons into the crowd and killed fourteen people.[20] Northern Ireland's Catholics were enraged.

What followed "Bloody Sunday" was a two-decade-long three-cornered campaign of terrorist violence in which thousands of people on both sides of the Republican–Loyalist division lost their lives. On one side, members of PIRA "active service" units assassinated representatives of the British political system. In 1984 PIRA even attempted to kill Prime Minister Margaret Thatcher. In both Northern Ireland itself as well as Great Britain PIRA set off bombs intended to kill on an indiscriminate basis during parades, marches, and other public ceremonies. Attempts were even made to attack British forces stationed in Germany and elsewhere on the continent.

Protestant or "loyalist" groups did not follow the examples set by Gandhi and Martin Luther King. The Ulster Defence Association (UDA), the Ulster Volunteer Force (UVF), and a succession of Protestant paramilitary organizations attacked Catholics in general and PIRA targets as they became available. Two generations of Northern Irish young people grew to adulthood in this atmosphere.

Despite a half dozen attempts over the years, involving power-sharing arrangements, by both the governments of Ireland and Great Britain to achieve an end to "The Troubles" it wasn't until 1994 that all parties to the struggle agreed to serious negotiations. PIRA leaders and their unionist counterparts agreed to a ceasefire as a precondition for entering the talks. These talks included the participation of all parties involved: the British and Irish governments, Northern Irish political parties, and leaders of the paramilitary organizations.[21]

The talks stretched out over more than four years. There were several setbacks along the way, including PIRA's 1996 decision to end its ceasefire. Eventually PIRA agreed to resume the ceasefire and the parties achieved a "Good Friday" peace agreement in April 1998, an arrangement that was subsequently approved by a substantial majority of voters in Northern Ireland. "The Troubles" had come to an end with a power-sharing agreement between Republicans and Unionists, Catholics and Protestants, while retaining Ulster's status as part of the United Kingdom.

Basic to the peace agreement was PIRA's willingness to end its campaign of violence and "decommission" its weapons. As a fighting organization PIRA's career had come to an end. It was superseded by its long-time political wing the Sinn Fein, which now as a political party competes at both provincial and British parliamentary elections. Why the change?

Gerry Adams and the rest of the PIRA leadership reached the conclusion they had taken the "armed struggle" about as far as it would go. They had not succeeded in escalating their terrorist activities into a wide-scale people's war, a general uprising. In fact, the people were exhausted. The British government showed no signs of giving up and leaving. The Irish government in Dublin expressed little sympathy for a continuation of the violence. All PIRA could do was explode more and more bombs but with less and less meaning. Sinn Fein could achieve more for the cause through political participation than PIRA could through the incessant combat. Perhaps in the long run Ireland could be reunited under republican auspices but at least in the immediate future "jaw, jaw," to quote Churchill, was better than "war, war."

From the specific to the general

So far we have discussed three cases in which groups employed terrorist tactics to achieve different political ends. The Montoneros sought revolution but provoked repression and defeat instead. The Algerian FLN won in the sense that terrorism aided in its pursuit of independence from France. PIRA underwent a transformation from paramilitarism to peaceful party politics after its leadership concluded that violence had become, or was on the verge of becoming, self-defeating. In the latter two cases, the FLN and PIRA, the groups involved and their leaders especially transformed themselves from violent opponents of the political order into its rulers. Algeria became a one-party state directed by the FLN's former leadership group. And in Northern Ireland Sinn Fein now shares political power at the provincial level with its former enemies.

The question we need to ask ourselves at this point is, just how representative are these three cases of how terrorist groups in general end their careers? We know already that the three were unusual in that they lasted longer than the average lifespan of such groups, years rather than months. Durability may mean the groups struck a nerve; they tapped a widely held sentiment among segments of the population that groups with more exotic agendas did not. Of course other explanations for group longevity come to mind. A contending explanation is that the groups' leaders were sufficiently cunning to have evaded detection by the relevant authorities until they represented a significant threat to the status quo. Still another account would be that the groups involved did not rise to the level of minor annoyance until they had gained a certain degree of momentum, before the authorities needed to take them seriously. The three explanations are not mutually contradictory by any means.

Among the more durable terrorist groups, how representative are the three cases we've reported? Fortunately this question does not have to be left dangling in the air. We can report the results of three studies that analyze how large numbers of terrorist groups ended their violent campaigns.

First, Dipak Gupta offers a theoretical overview of the rise and decline of terrorist movements.[22] Gupta's effort represents a natural history, with terrorist "movements" going through a beginning, middle, and end. For Gupta the birth of a movement involves the formation of a dissident group by a small band of strongly committed individuals. The grievances that the dissidents exploit already exist in the relevant population (e.g., ethnic group). It is the group that gives voice to them. Political "entrepreneurs" mobilize a community of followers by providing them with a narrative to justify their struggle as well as a sense of direction. At this stage, the group leadership develops an organizational structure. If at this point the dissident group confronts a situation in which 1) it is unable to create a mass following; and 2) there exists a vast asymmetry in power between the group and the authority it intends to challenge, there is a probability that the group will turn to terrorism.

Terrorist attacks may or may not attract an expanding base of supporters. In those cases in which the terrorist does expand it is usually the result of an interaction. Gupta, like many other analysts, assigns particular importance to the authorities. If they overreact by striking at the terrorist group's would-be constituency or commit other conspicuous blunders, the authorities will help the group expand its base of followers and recruit a new generation of members.

Over time though there are a number of factors that cause the group to de-escalate its terrorist operations. For Gupta these attenuating factors include the inability of the group to overcome the authorities' resort to overwhelming force and the unwillingness of society in general to tolerate a certain level of oppositional violence. When the latter reaches too high a level and when the government improves its tactics, the terrorist group will spiral downwards.

The result of this configuration is the death of the terrorist group or at least the end of its terrorist phase. Gupta's theoretical analysis relies heavily on work devoted to the rise and decline of social and political protest movements. Let us now turn our attention to studies that rely on the accumulation of empirical data on the ends of hundreds of terrorist groups.

The second study, conducted by Seth Jones and Martin Libicki for the Rand Corporation, investigates 648 terrorist groups active between 1968 and 2006.[23] Their data are drawn from Rand's own collection that dates back to the early years of the current "Age of Terrorism." The third, carried out by Audrey Cronin of the National Defense University, relies on data compiled by MIPT (the Memorial Institute for the Study of Terrorism in Oklahoma City). From this database Cronin analyzes the conduct of some 457 organizations active over the same period.[24] There is some overlap between the Rand and MIPT databases. Both studies recognize that terrorist groups typically meet their ends or suffer defeats through a combination of different factors. Nevertheless, there are central tendencies on which both studies focus. And both note as well the existence of some groups that continued to persist after 2006.

Based upon the frequency of their occurrence, Jones and Libicki identify five major ways terrorist groups have ended their careers in violence (1968–2006): policing, military force, splintering, politics, or victory (see Figure 2.1). I need to mention two more caveats. First, they exclude 244 groups active after 2006 and they also do not consider 136 groups that "splintered" (suffered from fragmentation) on the grounds that the various splinters continued to engage in terrorism.

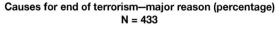

Causes for end of terrorism—major reason (percentage)
N = 433

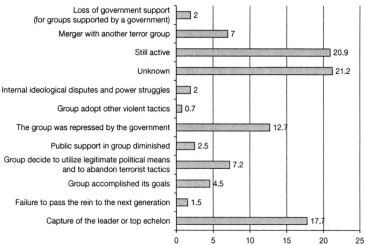

Figure 2.1 How terrorist groups end.

Source: Seth Jones and Martin Libicki, *How Terrorist Groups End* (Santa Monica, CA: Rand Corporation, 2008), p. 19.

With these limitations in mind Jones and Libicki report the surprising infrequency with which military force brought an end to terrorism (see above). They argue this outcome is the result of the fact that military force is typically a blunt instrument, while terrorist groups usually consist of small bands operating on a clandestine basis. In 1979, for example, over 50,000 Italian troops were deployed to locate the whereabouts of Aldo Moro, the former prime minister, who had been kidnapped by the Red Brigades. The military failed and Moro was later executed after having been held in captivity for fifty-five days.

On the other hand, conventional police work proved much more successful (see Figure 2.1). Jones and Libicki contend policing is better calibrated to responding to the kinds of challenges posed by small bands of terrorists operating in urban environments, situations in which knowing the neighborhoods, tapping informants, and other conventional forms of police work are exceptionally useful. In producing this finding Jones and Libicki have, perhaps accidently, jumped into the bear pit of political controversy. Waging a "war on terrorism" certainly suggests the deployment of large-scale military forces. How else are wars fought?

But by stressing the effectiveness of policing the authors suggest that terrorist activity resembles crime rather than war, at least under most circumstances.[25] If Jones and Libicki's finding holds up then we probably ought not to think of most conflicts involving terrorism to be a "war," reserving the term for armed conflicts between states or ones between large-scale insurgencies of one type or another.

Also, rather surprisingly, a high proportion of terrorist campaigns ended (see above) with the groups involved undergoing a transformation from violence to politics: the adage to the effect that "once a terrorist, always a terrorist" does not appear to be borne out by the evidence. There is an abundance of easily accessible cases in which terrorist groups abandoned violence for the partisan political arena. For instance, until the end of the apartheid regime in South Africa the ANC developed a group, the Spear of the Nation, which carried out a number of terrorist attacks on white targets, symbols of racial supremacy especially. Following South Africa's transition to majority rule in 1994, the ANC became the country's ruling political party and its leader Nelson Mandela won the Nobel Peace Prize for his efforts to shepherd this transition and avoid an inter-racial bloodbath.

The South African case is hardly unique. Over 40 percent of the episodes included in Jones and Libicki's data set ended as a consequence of groups turning away from terrorism and towards a more normal political life. Unfortunately, and as we will see later on in the discussion, it is possible for the relationship to go the other way, from party politics to terrorist violence. It is also possible for various groups to practice both electoral politics and terrorism simultaneously. In Lebanon, for example, Hezbollah (the Party of God) successfully participates in national election campaigns while, at the same time, staging terrorist attacks on Israeli targets from time to time.[26] Political parties that develop "military wings" seem especially inclined to launch terrorist campaigns at the same time their candidates campaign for public office.

For those who have been drawn to terrorism and its study by al-Qaeda and its mass casualty attacks on civilian targets during the 1990s and first decade of the twenty-first century, these results must seem implausible. Terrorism though has a long history, much of it involving groups with clear-cut political agendas, not al-Qaeda's apocalyptic religious visions. If we view things from this perspective, links between the use of terrorism and other forms of political expression, death by politics, become more understandable.

In about 10 percent of the cases included in the Jones and Libicki database the groups succeeded in achieving their objectives.[27] These successes though require some qualification. Jones and Libicki list the

Armenian Secret Army for the Liberation of Armenia and the Action Front for the Liberation of the Baltic Countries as victorious. There is a problem of cause and effect here. It is true that the three Baltic states (Latvia, Estonia, and Lithuania) and Armenia became independent as the Soviet Union disintegrated in the few years following 1989. But what these miniscule terrorist bands had to do with it remains to be seen. It is true that these groups were active before the Soviet Union collapsed but it requires a willful suspension of disbelief to conclude they had anything to do with the collapse beyond applauding when it occurred.

Tactical successes rather than strategic ones seem more likely the outcome of terrorist operations. Israel's decision to withdraw from southern Lebanon in 2000, for example, was strongly influenced by a spasm of martyrdom operations, in conjunction with guerrilla-style efforts, staged by Hezbollah militants.

The third study: Audrey Cronin, a professor and analyst at the National Defense University, has developed her own data set on how terrorist groups end. As with Jones and Libicki, Cronin's principal concern is with the defeat of al-Qaeda. Like the former, she believes that past experiences with terrorism will prove useful in helping al-Qaeda's opponents bring about the group's demise—one way or another. To accept this outlook is to suggest that al-Qaeda is not unique. Despite its network form of organization, its use of the Internet, and its religious fanaticism al-Qaeda's activities are sufficiently similar to make comparisons useful to the forces of order.

To this end, Cronin derives her understanding of how terrorist groups end from the experiences of 457 groups active from 1968 that meet two criteria: 1) the groups must have attacked civilian, as opposed to military, targets and have attacked people rather than just property; and 2) the groups in question must have sustained their operations for more than a few days. She excludes short-lived groups, in other words.[28] Cronin confines her data analysis to a limited number of variables: outcomes involving either success or failure; the groups' lifespan; and whether or not they engaged in negotiations with their adversaries. Plainly, Cronin is most interested in the effects of negotiations on the abandonment of terrorism.

At this point in the commentary our purpose is best served in reporting her principal findings. First, most terrorist groups fail to achieve their goals. Only twenty-nine groups (6.4 percent), Cronin discovers, achieved whatever it was they were seeking. Failure or defeat was then the most common result. Second, the chances of terrorist groups getting what they wanted or most of what they wanted were enhanced if they were durable and if they entered into negotiations with the authorities.

A negotiated solution, as was achieved in Northern Ireland, whereby the terrorist organization abandons violence in exchange for winning some of its objectives, an opportunity to come in from the cold and participate in the political process, certainly seems to be an attractive solution—especially for democratic regimes. Negotiations have their limitations, however. The sociologist Christopher Hewitt analyzed the effects of negotiating with terrorists many years ago.[29] Hewitt found a significant decline in violence while talks were under way. But if the negotiations failed for whatever reason and were broken off, the result was that terrorism resumed at a more lethal level than before they began. He detected another consideration. If leaders of terrorist groups engaged in negotiations concede too much in the eyes of certain followers they may break away, create their own independent groups, and launch new terrorist campaigns. A rose by any other name . . . Terrorist groups are typically extremist in outlook so that for many members concessions to the authorities will be seen as treason or betrayal of the cause and will cause them to exit the organization in pursuit of a renewed militancy. The tale of the Real IRA following the Good Friday Agreement illustrates the problem, as does the biography of Michael Collins, the IRA hero of the 1920s who was assassinated by his own followers for negotiating a compromise with the British. Diehards, in other words, may find anything other than total victory unacceptable. In fact, they may regard a compromise agreement as a renewed call to arms.

In a series of three publications Audrey Cronin provides us with a set of outcomes about the possible endings of terrorist groups.[30] From her perspective, how may terrorist groups conclude their careers in violence?

First, she mentions decapitation. A group may dissolve or at least lose its momentum if the leader or leaders are killed or captured. In some instances though, this may have the opposite effect or no effect at all. For instance, in Italy the Red Brigades actually gained strength and became more lethal following the arrest and prosecution of its "historic nucleus" in the mid-1970s. If the group is able to transform its erstwhile leader into a martyr then his or her death actually may be a benefit to the group. The killing of wheelchair-bound Sheik Yassin, founder and spiritual guide of Hamas, by Israelis, probably reaped considerable publicity benefits for the group. And, at least in the short term, Hamas became more murderous after his death.

The story may be different though for a group dominated by a cunning and charismatic figure. In Peru, for example, the Shining Path has never represented the same menace it did before the capture of its leader Abimael Guzman. The Japanese group Aum Shinrikyo completely fell apart after the arrest of its head, the self-styled demigod Shoko Asahara.

Second, Cronin identifies negotiations as another possible end for terrorist groups. We ordinarily think of negotiated settlements in connection with international wars or with major internal wars. Terrorist conflicts involving challenges to an incumbent regime are often called "asymmetric" because of the enormous difference in power between the parties involved. Are negotiated settlements possible under these circumstances? What is involved?

Disparity in power may not be an insuperable barrier. After all, during World War II the United States, a country that had over 11 million people in uniform at the time, engaged in tacit negotiations with the New York Mafia over its control over the Brooklyn Navy Yard. In exchange for labor peace, the US Justice Department was willing to grant certain concessions to Charles "Lucky" Luciano and his sub-bosses who controlled the dockworkers' union. Is it any wonder that the "honored society" resumed its prominence in Sicilian life following the island's liberation from Fascist and Nazi control by the Allies in the summer of 1943?[31] If the group is able to inflict damage beyond what the stronger side is willing to accept, negotiations become serious possibilities.

Third, as Cronin and other analysts have noted, terrorism may prove successful, in the sense that its practitioners get what they want. What is it though that they want? In the short term at least the answers are well known: revenge, publicity, concessions, e.g., release of prisoners, etc.[32] The achievement of long-term strategic aims is another story though. For now we prefer just to observe that, as David Rapoport notes, terrorist groups managed to achieve their strategic aims most often during the post-World War II era of national independence struggles in Africa, the Middle East, and Asia. Terrorist violence proved most successful as the sun set on the vast European empires.

Cronin mentions failure as an additional possible outcome. By failure she has in mind forms of defeat not directly related to the authorities' efforts. Rather Cronin refers to defeats that are largely self-inflicted. Terrorist groups may lose popular support in a number of ways. Their ideas may lose their vitality; they may come to seem irrelevant even to their nominal constituents. It was hard for Marxist–Leninist groups to sustain themselves following the collapse of the Berlin Wall. Islamist groups that carried out indiscriminate attacks on a wedding party at a hotel in Jordan or foreign tourists in Egypt managed to cause a popular backlash against themselves and consequently lost "contact" with the people. Such loss of contact may be inherent in the way many terrorist groups need to operate. If they operate on a clandestine basis, fearful of pursuit by the authorities, terrorists are likely over time to develop a distorted view of reality: the result of social isolation. To make matters worse, terrorist groups, like extremist groups in general, possess ideas and ideologies so abstract and confusing that they are unable to express them with any clarity to the public. Also, their threats may be so blood-curdling the groups may lose whatever attraction they had at the beginning of their careers in violence. And, like extremist political parties, terrorist bands are highly susceptible to fragmentation, often followed by dissolution.

Not uncommonly, as Cronin points out, terrorists lack the ability to recruit new generations of militants and supporters. Often we are dealing with terrorist activity linked to a generational rebellion.[33] In the Western world, for example, the Vietnam War set off massive youth protests by students and other young people who were in a sense rebelling against the ways and wars of their parents. In Italy, Germany, and the United States these protests led to the formation of terrorist groups by youths persuaded the "system" was beyond repair. Once the war ended and the emotions it had unleashed dissipated, new, younger generations lost interest and recruitment became progressively harder.

Last on Cronin's list of causes for the end of terrorist groups are repression and reorientation. We have already mentioned the problems linked to a state's repressive apparatus and will expand this account shortly. For the moment though we might simply comment that repression —the use of coercive techniques—to end terrorism need not be confined to work by the authorities. Private groups and organizations may pursue this objective as well. Unlike government agencies in democratic settings, Latin American "death squads," Pinkertons (in nineteenth-century America), Blackwater and the Mahdi Army (in twenty-first-century Iraq), and other private militias are not bound by the rule of law.

Cronin also thinks that groups may end their terrorist campaigns by reorienting themselves. In some cases the terrorism persists but its purpose changes, from politics to crime. Groups with ostensible political agendas abandon them in favor of straightforward money-making. In Northern Ireland remnants of the IRA have turned to bank robbery not as a means of advancing the republican cause but as a way of filling their pockets. In the Philippines the Abu Sayyaf band, nominally a group with ties to al-Qaeda, kidnaps foreign tourists for cash. Before his demise in Iraq, Abu Nidal used his Fatah Revolutionary Council to carry out "hits" on whatever target a state or organization was willing to pay him to do so. In Colombia the FARC, its revolutionary objectives largely a thing of the past, now devotes most of its energies to the drug business. In fact, as Jessica Stern has pointed out, religious rhetoric notwithstanding, the spiritual guides of various jihadi groups in Pakistan are more concerned with material benefits than their places in Paradise.[34]

Corruption is one thing but it is hardly the only way terrorist groups reorient themselves. Instead of switching from politics to crime, they may change tactics from terrorism to some other type of violence. To this point in our discussion we have treated terrorist groups as stand-alone units. This need not be the case, however. Terrorism may be one tactic among several in the repertoire of violent organizations. Today, Taliban insurgents in Pakistan, for example, carry out suicide attacks on civilian targets in Islamabad and other major cities while simultaneously staging guerrilla operations against government targets throughout Waziristan and other tribal areas. Some, more flexible, insurgent groups may reorient or adapt their tactics to suit the needs of the moment.

We have relied on a somewhat different database than Jones and Libicki, and Cronin to produce our own frequency distribution on how terrorist groups have met their ends. Our collection of 433 groups constitutes a merger of data compiled by the University of Haifa's national security studies center, the US Department of State's Patterns of Global Terrorism Project, Schmid and Jongman's *Political Terrorism: A New Guide to Actors, Authors, Concepts, Data Bases, Theories, and Literature*, and the MIPT collection.[35] In addition, we made an effort to include groups that were active, at one point or another, over the entire twentieth century and the first half decade of the twenty-first (1900–2006). Given the wider time frame encompassed in our collection we might mention some attributes of the groups that were included.

First, we are dealing with groups strongly animated by left-wing and right-wing ideologies as well as nationalist causes. Over 40 percent of these groups were left-wing revolutionary in character. Some 16 percent identified themselves as on the right, e.g., fascist, neo-fascist, and neo-Nazi. National independence and separatism represented the fundamental outlook of another 20 percent of the population. Religious concerns were the dominant perspectives in only 11 percent of the groups active in the more than a century of terrorist violence included in the study. Among other things the data very likely underestimate the role of religion in the contemporary manifestations of terrorism. These data also introduce an element of nostalgia into the commentary. Causes that once drove groups to launch terrorist operations have in recent years lost much of their appeal.

Second, the data exhibit a "pro-democratic" bias. Terrorist groups were rarely present in such authoritarian settings as ruling monarchies, autocracies and theocracies. They were most prevalent in the democracies; parliamentary or presidential made virtually no difference.

Third, the groups included in the database were hardly isolated. Pluralities had relationships both with other terrorist groups and with sympathetic countries. Rather than being national or international pariahs, significant numbers of the groups enjoyed state sponsorship and ties to like-minded organizations.

At this point it does no harm to reiterate that, as with the other analyses, identifying how terrorist groups end is a matter of choosing a central tendency rather than making an "either or" decision.

We are dealing, to repeat, with a population of some 433 groups that were active between 1900 and 2006. Please notice that of that number close to 21 percent (or ninety-one groups) were still active in 2006. This is a figure of some significance because it includes al-Qaeda and the various units that compose most of its worldwide network (e.g., al-Qaeda in the Arabian Peninsula). Hezbollah and Hamas are certainly still active at the end of the first decade of the twenty-first century. So our database inevitably under-represents religiously motivated organizations. How did the remaining 342 groups though conclude their terrorist operations? Consistent with Jones and Libicki as well as Cronin, we can report (see Figure 2.2) that only a small percentage of them managed to achieve their goals. Terrorism in and of itself was rarely a winning tactic. It was also very rare for terrorist groups to switch tactics and pursue their goals via other types of violence, e.g., guerrilla warfare. Some groups "ended" by merging or subordinating themselves with other groups. The terrorist violence persisted but under new auspices.

A more than negligible percentage of the groups were able to transform themselves into nonviolent political organizations, political parties in particular. We were unable to identify the end of slightly more than a fifth of the groups, a highly significant proportion of our still-active population. Based on the Jones and Libicki, and Cronin findings, we might infer that negotiations or bargaining were important factors in bringing an end to these terrorist groups.

On the other hand, our frequency distribution certainly suggests there is something to be said for the use of force, at least on a selective basis. Government repression explains more than 10 percent of the group endings. But we should quickly note that figure is exceeded by the number of groups whose terrorist activities were ended by the capture or killing of the groups' leadership cadre. In other words, the selective use of force seems to be a more productive way of ending terrorist activity than less discriminating types of action.

The issue of "decapitation" or "targeted killing" has drawn considerable attention. The two are not the same. Decapitation may refer to both killing as well as arrest and detention. Studies have produced a mixture of findings. Several studies report negative results at least insofar as al-Qaeda and other religious groups are concerned. Jenna

Jordan examined the effectiveness of targeted killings across a wide spectrum of groups active from the late 1960s forward. Mohammed Hafez and Joseph Hatfield measured the impact of targeted killings carried out by the Israelis during the Al-Aqsa Intifada. Austin Long analyzed the impact of such assassinations in the struggle over Iraq.[36]

On the other hand, some investigators have come to more positive judgments about the benefits of decapitation. Alex Wilner explored the results of targeted killings in Afghanistan and the Federally Administered Tribal Areas (FATA) of Pakistan. Edward Kaplan and his co-authors considered the impact of such killings and other measures employed by the Israelis during the Al-Aqsa Intifada. They did so from a somewhat different perspective than Hafez and Hatfield.[37]

For Jordan the two key variables are religion and longevity. For Long the crucial factor is "institutionalization." Targeted killings have an impact on reducing the level of terrorism for relatively young and small groups dominated by charismatic leaders. Long-lasting groups and ones claiming religious inspiration appear unaffected by such killings. The same applies to groups that have achieved a significant level of "institutionalization," i.e., terrorist groups that have developed regular patterns of leadership selection, decision-making, and recruitment. To illustrate, Long compared AQI with its various competitors and opponents in the struggle to dominate Baghdad. At best, Jordan and Long found that for groups exhibiting these defining characteristics, targeted killings offer only some short-term disruptions.

Hafez and Hatfield measured the frequency of suicide bombings and other attacks carried out by Hamas, PIJ, al-Aqsa Martyrs' Brigades, and other Palestinian groups during the 2000–2004 uprising before and after Israeli forces carried out targeted killings. Their general finding is that these assassinations had no effect in either direction. The frequency of terrorist attacks neither increased nor decreased as a result of the killings.

The other studies point in a different direction. Alex Wilner maintains there are metrics other than a decline in the frequency of terrorist attacks that can be used to measure the effectiveness of targeted killings. He sought to examine the consequences of these killings for the fighting in Afghanistan and reports as follows:

> Overall levels of violence however are only a minor part of the analysis. The data also reveal changes in Taliban professionalism following targeted killings. For the two most sophisticated forms of violence (IEDs and suicide bombings), the aggregate data suggest a decrease in professionalism and an increase in failure rates.[38]

Wilner goes on to point out that following targeted killings of Taliban leaders, at different echelons, there has also been a significant shift in targeting, with "soft" civilian targets replacing "hard" military and police ones.

Kaplan and his co-authors stress the difference between decapitation and targeted killings. Nonlethal apprehension, arrest, or capture, may have certain advantages over killings. For one, this technique is less likely to transform the erstwhile leader or cadre into a martyr whose name can be used to justify further attacks. Arrest and detention are also less likely to arouse popular anger and calls for revenge. Indeed this is the principal finding of Kaplan and his co-authors. In the Israeli–Palestinian case they assert there was a radical decline in suicide bombings during the Al-Aqsa Intifada not because of the targeted killings but because, thanks largely to human intelligence, the Israeli security agencies were able to arrest and detain potential suicides before they left on their missions. Decapitation succeeded while targeted killings did not.

Our results (see Figure 2.2) reinforce the view that decapitation, meaning apprehension especially, provides a major benefit in disrupting terrorist operations. Various caveats should be mentioned (see above) but the benefits appear to be substantial.

By our calculations at least self-destruction does not seem to be a major way in which the groups ended. If we cluster "internal divisions" together with an inability of the groups to produce a new generation of militants, we are hardly explaining many endings. And if we add to this

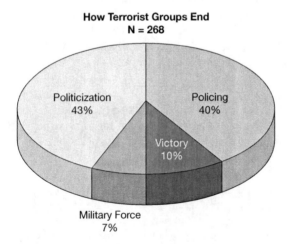

Figure 2.2 Causes for the end of terrorism—major reasons.

figure a decline in public support, which is surely related to the groups' public presentations of themselves, the cumulative result still does not seem all that meaningful.

If terrorism rarely succeeds in achieving, what do its perpetrators hope it will achieve? Why do it? One answer suggested by a few analysts is group solidarity.[39] People join terrorist groups not because they have any reasonable expectations that it will be able to achieve its objectives, but rather out of a need for association with like-minded individuals. This may be true but it does not explain membership in a group whose modus operandi is attacking unarmed civilians. Another explanation is that those who found and lead terrorist groups rarely have been exposed to social science methodology, probability theory in particular, and consequently are unable to calculate their chances of success. Speaking of social science methodology, perhaps we have posed the question incorrectly. Instead of suggesting that success is rare among groups who have launched terrorist campaigns already, we ought to ask whether among a population of extremist groups are those that employ terrorist violence any more or less successful than those who do not?

Since defeat is the most common result for those groups who use the tactic, we think it makes sense to devote Chapter 3 to this subject. We intend to investigate how and why terrorist groups are not likely to get what they say they want.

3 Defeat

Today the fear of terrorism is widespread. Almost on a daily basis the mass media display the effects of suicide bombings in Iraq, Afghanistan, Pakistan, and elsewhere. At a Washington conference in April 2010, US President Obama identified the prospects of terrorists acquiring nuclear weapons or nuclear material as the single greatest menace to international security facing the world. Television networks often show pictures of terrorist luminaries and even failed suicide bombers, striking either threatening or bewildered poses for audiences to contemplate. On the Internet, rather than seeking clandestinity, terrorist groups often "strut their stuff" by using their websites to issue press releases along with blood-curdling threats against potential targets. Boasting is not uncommon. For the ghoulish and blood-thirsty, a few key strokes will permit them to view beheadings of Daniel Pearl, Nicholas Berg, and other terrorist captives.

These messages frequently leave citizens in the Western democracies with the impression that a so-called "Islamo-fascism" represents a threat equivalent to those posed by Nazi Germany, Imperial Japan, or the Soviet Union at the height of their powers. Is this perception accurate? To what extent does it conform to reality? Or, are we dealing with a lot of sound and fury signifying not all that much?

In this chapter we propose to answer these questions in the following manner. Initially we intend to comment on some recent work focused on the outcomes of terrorist campaigns. Next we analyze several cases to illustrate the various ways in which terrorist groups have been defeated—by the military, police, vigilantes, leadership decapitation, or by self-destruction.

The UCLA analyst Max Abrahams places himself in the middle of a debate that has been raging for some time between those, like Alan Dershowitz, who believe that terrorism works, in the sense that the groups that use it are likely to achieve their objectives (in Dershowitz's case this means largely calling attention and winning publicity for the cause) and those like John Mueller who conclude that despite all the sound and fury terrorism signifies very little.[1] There is a third position to which Abrahams calls our attention. In this view, as Herbert Simon would have it, we should be alert to the distinction between "substantive" and "procedural" rationality. Terrorist groups may achieve procedural rationality in successfully figuring how to go about detonating bombs in the Moscow subway system (2010) in the hope of killing large numbers of passengers. The same may be said in regard to Aum Shinrikyo's dispersion of sarin gas in Tokyo's subways in 1995. But in neither case have the perpetrators achieved substantive rationality. The likelihood of the groups involved reaching their ostensible goals, i.e., an independent Chechnya or accelerating an end to the world, seems unlikely.

Equipped with Abrahams' theoretical insights, let us turn our attention to his own substantive findings. He considers the outcomes achieved by twenty-eight foreign terrorist organizations identified by the US state department since 2001 (Table 3.1). Abrahams points out that most of these groups had been active since 1978 and a majority had engaged in terrorism since the 1960s, ample time, he believes, for them to have achieved their objectives. His basic point though is that they very rarely do.

Of the twenty-eight groups included in the collection Abrahams finds that only four managed to achieve either limited or partial success in achieving their ostensible goals. In two instances terrorism scored total successes. Among the four partial or limited success stories, the Tamil Tigers were destroyed by the Sri Lankan military in 2009—after the article's publication—and the FARC has essentially become a criminal organization involved in the drug business, although, to be fair, it does occupy some isolated regions of Colombia. Hamas and Palestinian Islamic Jihad (PIJ) achieved a limited success in 2006 in that their use of suicide attacks—martyrdom operations—did accelerate the Israelis' decision to withdraw from the Gaza Strip. Abrahams also calculates that al-Qaeda's attacks against American forces and their allies in Iraq caused the United States to stage a limited withdrawal from the Persian Gulf region. But of course this is not entirely true. If anything the phased withdrawal of the US military from Iraq has had more to do with al-Qaeda's defeat than American failure.

The two cases of total terrorist success Abrahams identifies were the efforts of Hezbollah to coerce the withdrawal of American and French peacekeeping forces from Lebanon in 1983 and the decision by the Israeli

Table 3.1 The outcome of terrorist campaigns

Group	Objective	Type	Main target	Outcome
Abu Nidal Organization	Destroy Israel	Maximalist	Civilian	No success
Abu Sayyaf Group	Establish Islamic state in Philippines	Maximalist	Civilian	No success
al-Qaeda	Expel the United States from Persian Gulf	Limited	Civilian	Limited success
al-Qaeda	Sever US–Israel relations	Idiosyncratic	Civilian	No success
al-Qaeda	Sever US–apostate relations	Idiosyncratic	Civilian	No success
al-Qaeda	Spare Muslims from "Crusader wars"	Idiosyncratic	Civilian	No success
Armed Islamic Group	Establish Islamic state in Algeria	Maximalist	Civilian	No success
Aum Shinrikyo	Establish utopian society in Japan	Maximalist	Civilian	No success
Egyptian Islamic Jihad	Establish Islamic state in Egypt	Maximalist	Civilian	No success
Fatherland and Liberty	Establish Basque state	Limited	Civilian	No success
Hamas	Establish state in historic Palestine	Maximalist	Civilian	Limited success
Hamas	Destroy Israel	Maximalist	Civilian	No success
Harakat ul-Mujahidin	Rule Kashmir	Limited	Military	No success
Harakat ul-Mujahidin	Eliminate Indian insurgents	Idiosyncratic	Military	No success
Hezbollah (Lebanese)	Expel peacekeepers	Limited	Military	Total success
Hezbollah (Lebanese)	Expel Israel	Limited	Military	Total success
Hezbollah (Lebanese)	Destroy Israel	Maximalist	Military	No success
Islamic Group	Establish Islamic state in Egypt	Maximalist	Civilian	No success
Islamic Jihad	Establish state in historic Palestine	Maximalist	Civilian	Limited success
Islamic Jihad	Destroy Israel	Maximalist	Civilian	No success
Islamic Movement of Uzbekistan	Establish Islamic state in Uzbekistan	Maximalist	Military	No success

Organization	Objective	Goal	Target	Outcome
Kach	Transfer Palestinians from Israel	Idiosyncratic	Civilian	No success
Kurdistan Workers' Party	Establish Kurdish state in Middle East	Limited	Civilian	No success
Kurdistan Workers' Party	Establish communism in Turkey	Maximalist	Civilian	No success
Mujahideen-e-Khalq	End clerical rule in Iran	Maximalist	Military	No success
National Liberation Army	Establish Marxism in Colombia	Maximalist	Civilian	No success
November 17	Establish Marxism in Greece	Maximalist	Civilian	No success
November 17	Sever US–Greek relations	Idiosyncratic	Civilian	No success
Palestine Liberation Front	Destroy Israel	Maximalist	Civilian	No success
People's Liberation Front	Establish Marxism in Turkey	Maximalist	Civilian	No success
People's Liberation Front	Sever US–Turkish relations	Idiosyncratic	Civilian	No success
Popular Front for the Liberation of Palestine (PFLP)	Destroy Israel	Maximalist	Civilian	No success
PFLP	Establish Marxist Palestine	Maximalist	Civilian	No success
PFLP-General Command	Destroy Israel	Maximalist	Military	No success
PFLP-General Command	Establish Marxist Palestine	Maximalist	Military	No success
Real Irish Republican Army	Establish Irish unification	Limited	Military	No success
Revolutionary Armed Forces of Colombia	Establish peasant rule in Colombia	Maximalist	Military	Limited success
Revolutionary Nuclei	Establish Marxism in Greece	Maximalist	Military	No success
Revolutionary Nuclei	Sever US–Greek relations	Idiosyncratic	Military	No success
Shining Path	Establish communism in Peru	Maximalist	Civilian	No success
Tamil Tigers	Establish Tamil state	Limited	Military	Partial success
United forces of Colombia	Eliminate left-wing insurgents	Idiosyncratic	Civilian	No success

Source: Max Abrahams, "Why Terrorism Does Not Work," *International Security* 31(2) (Fall 2006): 49–50.

government to leave its "security zone" in the southern part of the country in 2000. Please notice though these were tactical achievements. Hezbollah's strategic goals are the destruction of Israel and the transformation of Lebanon into a Shiite-dominated Islamic Republic. Neither objective seems any closer to realization than when Sheik Nasrallah, the group's leader, originally articulated them.

Abrahams does not include the case in his analysis but we might mention the March 2004 morning commuter train bombings in Madrid. These attacks, carried out by al-Qaeda-linked Moroccan immigrants to Spain, influenced the results of the country's national elections scheduled for a few days after the attacks. The Socialists, under the leadership of Jose-Luis Zapatero, defeated the Popular Party, their conservative opponents, and made good on their pledge to withdraw Spanish troops from Iraq: the outcome the terrorists had hoped to achieve. (Admittedly the election results might have been different had not the Populist government of Jose Aznar lied to the public by initially blaming Basque separatists for the attack.)[2]

The message these accounts convey is that terrorist campaigns very rarely achieve the long-term goals or strategic objectives of those groups waging them. On those few occasions when the groups succeed it is almost always in the realm of their tactical aims. We may say the same in connection with contemporary terrorism's most compelling weapon of choice: the suicide bomb attack.

These attacks or "martyrdom operations" for Salafist jihadi appear successful in at least two senses of the word. First, they enhance the capacity of terrorist groups to kill people.[3] For those groups interested in maximizing the number of deaths and injuries per attack, suicide bombings represent improvements over previously used techniques. The suicide bomber has the flexibility to move from one place to another until he or she finds a locale likely to cause the most damage and kill the most people. In addition, those terrorists planning the operations do not have to worry about escape routes and threats posed to their own security by the bombers falling into the hands of their enemies.

Second, if copying the behavior is the sincerest form of flattery, then suicide attacks have been eminently successful. Martyrdom operations began in Lebanon under Shiite Muslim auspices in 1983 and subsequently spread to Sunni groups in the Middle East and elsewhere in the Muslim world. Moreover, groups acting in the name of nationalism, e.g., the Tamil Tigers in Sri Lanka, The Kurdish Workers' Party (PKK) in Turkey, and other secular causes, have adopted the technique.[4]

In terms of process rationality suicide bombings certainly make sense, at least for the moment. Substantive rationality may be another story, however. The record suggests that suicide bombing campaigns have failed, so far, to achieve any of the long-term goals of those groups that have launched them. If, for example, suicide bombings played a role in persuading the Israelis to withdraw from South Lebanon and the Gaza Strip, they have not moved Hezbollah, Hamas, or PIJ any steps closer to their long-term goal of destroying the Jewish state. They have though made the prospects of a negotiated settlement to the protracted conflict much more difficult. To that extent they may share a basic interest with right-wing Israeli governments that themselves show a very limited interest in reaching such an agreement with the Palestinian authorities. It is, no doubt, far-fetched and certainly a bit facetious, but in this instance, right-wing Israeli governments might very well have an incentive to provide these radical Jihadi organizations with stipends—state-support in other words—to maintain their self-defeating terrorist operations.

Suicide bombings may not be the last word in terrorism techniques. The spread of short-range missiles and the technology to build them to terrorist organizations will likely make it possible for the wealthier and more innovative groups to replace suicide attacks with these standoff weapons and achieve the same effects with less gore. Hezbollah and Hamas appear to be in the process of undergoing these changes.

Defeat is far and away the most common result of political groups that launch terrorist campaigns, but not all defeats are the same. Some require little effort on the part of the authorities attempting to deal with the threat. The arrest of a few key leaders is sufficient to do the job. The demise of Action Directe in France and the Silent Brotherhood in the United States did not require much more effort than that required to apprehend a gang of Parisian or Seattle bank robbers. At the other end of the spectrum are situations that place severe strains on the forces of order. Some cases seem to require the mobilization of a country's military and intelligence apparatus. Israel's largely successful repression of the Al-Aqsa Intifada in the several years following its outbreak in the fall of 2000 would be a case in point. Below are a few cases to illustrate the various ways terrorist groups suffer defeat.

The Tamil Tigers in Sri Lanka

The long-term conflict between the Sri Lankan government and the secession-minded Liberation Tigers of Tamil Eelam (LTTE) clearly represents a case in which the authorities had to exercise a maximum effort to bring about the latter's defeat. From the onset of the LTTE's insurgency in 1983 to its ultimate or apparently ultimate defeat in 2009 some thousands of Sri Lankans, both Sinhalese and Tamil, lost their lives as the result of terrorist bombings, guerrilla skirmishes, and large-scale fighting. The conflict displaced hundreds of thousands of Tamils.[5] Prominent officials including Indian Prime Minister Rajiv Gandhi were assassinated.

The conflict's origins may be traced to the period of British rule on what was then called Ceylon. During the colonialist era Britain's administrators tended to award government jobs and extend preferential treatment to the country's minority Hindu population of Tamils, selected by the British to serve as the "state people." Significant numbers of Tamils (who came to be known as "estate" Tamils) had been brought to Ceylon in the nineteenth century to work on tea plantations. They came from a region of southeastern India, now the state of Tamil Nadu. The majority of Sri Lanka's Tamil community lives in the northeast corner of the country. The majority population on the island, then as now, was composed of the Buddhist Sinhalese.

When the British left Sri Lanka in 1948 they bequeathed a democratic constitution that provided for majority rule. Sinhalese political leaders took the opportunity to overturn the preferential treatment accorded to the Tamils by the British. One of the first means by which the Sinhalese-dominated parliament achieved this objective was by essentially disfranchising the "estate Tamils." Legally they were then treated as nonvoting residents.[6] The effect was to reduce still further the influence of the Tamil minority in the Sri Lankan parliament. Other discriminatory measures followed.

"The 'Sinhala Only' Act of 1956, making Sinhalese the sole official language, was the key tipping point ... The language issue directly affected two core institutions: the state bureaucracy and education."[7] The impact of the Act was a dramatic reduction of the Tamil presence in public employment and in higher education. Tamils tended to feel humiliated and largely helpless. The Sinhalese, on the other hand, felt they had redressed a wrong, namely their own discrimination at the hands of the British and their Tamil beneficiaries.

Other discriminatory measures followed. Among other things, Buddhism was made the state's official religion. In effect, the Tamils were demoted to the status, politically and economically, of second-class citizens. Their initial response to their diminished circumstance was non-violent protest and party political organization. These tactics produced very modest improvements in the status of the Tamils. By the 1970s the conflict escalated, from the demand for equality of status to the demand for a separate state of Tamil Eelam (Tamil Homeland), and from relatively peaceful protest to outbreaks of violence.[8]

During the 1970s there was a proliferation of Tamil political organizations. Some were founded as political parties while others, known as the Tamil Five, were groups strongly committed to secession and with a clear willingness to use violent means to achieve this goal. The most important of the political parties was the Tamil United Liberation Front (TULF) established in 1972. The most significant of the radical groups was the Tamil National Tigers (TNT) led by a charismatic figure, Vellupillai Prabhakaran. Originally the Tigers represented the armed and youth wing of TULF. But by 1978 the group split from its parent political party and renamed itself the Liberation Tigers of Tamil Eelam (LTTE). Its goal was a separate state and its method was armed insurrection against the government in Colombo. And the use of terrorism became one of the principal tools in its arsenal.

LTTE's campaign was aided by a massive outbreak of communal violence that occurred in the summer of 1983. Anti-Tamil rioting broke out in Colombo after the LTTE had ambushed and killed thirteen Sinhalese soldiers. The military put their mutilated bodies on display. The sight inflamed masses of Sinhalese witnesses. Over several days that followed mobs in and around Colombo, the Sri Lankan capital, attacked Tamils on an indiscriminate basis. Tamil businesses and homes were burned down and over 300 Tamils were killed. Approximately 100,000 Tamils were left homeless and another 200,000–250,000 fled across the narrow Palk Strait to the state of Tamil Nadu in India.[9] The government may very well have been complicit in these attacks. The rioters evidently possessed voter lists that identified the Tamils' places of residence. And Sinhalese soldiers participated in the riots.

The 1983 rioting (there had been outbreaks of communal violence earlier in Sri Lanka's history) had a transformative effect. Before the riots the LTTE had consisted of about 600 fighters, after them its ranks swelled to more than ten thousand. Prabhakaran, the LTTE leader, was not only charismatic but exceptionally ruthless as well. He systematically went about crushing the competing Tamil secessionist groups so that the LTTE could claim a monopoly over the armed struggle. The Sri Lankan government unintentionally made the situation more flammable by using the constitution to bar any political party that advocated secession, thereby excluding the TULF from parliament.[10]

In the several years following the 1983 riots the LTTE evolved into what one analyst refers to as a "full spectrum" insurgency. With financial support coming from Tamil supporters in Tamil Nadu and Diaspora groups in Europe and North America, the LTTE developed an elaborate organizational format. Below Prabhakaran and his immediate advisers were military and political wings. The former came to consist of an elite regiment of fighters, an amphibious group of Sea Tigers, an airborne force of Air Tigers, an intelligence apparatus, and the Black Tigers— men and women prepared to carry out suicide attacks on targets designated by Prabhakaran.

The Black Tigers are of particular interest. The LTTE here clearly emulated groups in the Middle East who adopted this terrorist technique, although in this instance there was no expectation of a heavenly reward for carrying out suicide attacks. During the ensuing two decades the Black Tigers (who wore amulets containing cyanide tablets around their neck to avoid being captured alive), including women known as "Birds of Paradise," carried out suicide attacks on three types of targets. The group targeted members of the Sinhalese-dominated Sri Lankan military. It assassinated prominent political leaders including the president of Sri Lanka and the prime minister of India. And the Tigers attacked civilians as well. In this regard, the most spectacular terrorist event was the bombing of the central Colombo bus station in April 1987 that killed 113 people.

In response the Sri Lankan government launched an offensive in LTTE-held territory, the Jaffna Peninsula, and killed large numbers of Tamil civilians. It was at this point that the Indian government intervened, at first by providing humanitarian relief to the beleaguered and displaced Tamils in Jaffna and then by pursuing peace negotiations. Seeking to win electoral support among the c.60 million Tamils in Tamil Nadu, Indian Prime Minister Rajiv Gandhi sought an agreement with the Sri Lankan government. The result of these discussions was an Accord that provided local autonomy for the Tamil areas of North and Northeast Sri Lanka, but within the context of Sri Lanka: no national independence. Furthermore, the Indian army was to replace Sri Lankan forces in July 1987 and enforce compliance with the Accord. The LTTE was to be disarmed without Prabhakaran's consent. Nor did the LTTE leader agree to abandon his demand for Tamil Eelam's complete independence.[11]

Instead of disarming, LTTE militants became engaged in a violent conflict with the Indian military. Over the next two years the fighting between the "Indian Peace-Keeping Forces" and the LTTE escalated. Indian intervention had been intended initially to protect the Tamil population from depredations at the hands of the Sri Lankan military. But by 1990 India found itself in a virtual war with the LTTE. As a consequence New Delhi decided to withdraw its forces, leaving the situation in worse condition than it had found it. Rajiv Gandhi was then repaid for his good offices by being assassinated. Two "Birds of Paradise" blew themselves up in Gandhi's presence while the prime minister was campaigning for voter support in Tamil Nadu (1991).

Gandhi was not the last prominent political figure to be killed in the conflict. In 1993 LTTE suicide bombers assassinated the Sri Lankan President Ranasinghe Premadassa. And the following year the former deputy leader of the LTTE, Mahattaya, was also murdered for allegedly betraying the cause and acting as an agent of the Indians and for seeking to remove Prabhakaran as its leader.

Throughout the remainder of the 1990s fighting between the Sri Lankan forces and the LTTE continued on and off, with periodic and short-lived truces. During this period the LTTE used the full repertoire of human and material resources at its disposal. Thanks to the philanthropy of Tamil groups in India and other parts of the world, the LTTE used its "navy" to attack Sri Lankan ships and employed its handful of planes to attack Sri Lankan targets on the ground. It conducted this fighting in addition to waging guerrilla attacks on the Sri Lankan military and terrorist attacks on both civilian and military targets.

In 2001 the LTTE changed its demand from a separate state to one of regional autonomy. The organization also declared a unilateral ceasefire to which the Sri Lankan government agreed and the following year both sides signed an agreement formalizing their commitment to the ceasefire. Norway, a neutral party, agreed to send monitors to make sure the agreement was kept. Over the next several years the Norwegians, later to be condemned as "salmon eaters" by the LTTE for their good offices, sponsored a series of peace negotiations. These failed, with the government in Oslo blaming the LTTE for the failures.

In 2005 voters elected a new Sri Lankan president, Mahinda Rajapaksa, who was committed to defeating the LTTE by military means.[12] The new president, an ardent defender of Buddhist nationalism and with the backing of the Buddhist clergy, in 2006 had the military launch a full-scale attack on sections of Sri Lanka under LTTE control. Tamil civilians were killed and displaced by the thousands. By the end of 2009 the LTTE was completely defeated and Prabhakaran ended his career by being shot and killed. The Sinhalese were jubilant. Crowds in Colombo poured into the streets to celebrate their victory.

The magnitude of the challenge posed by the LTTE was substantially more than that of a small band of terrorists carrying out bombing attacks on civilian targets from time to time. Instead the Tamil organization represented a full-scale insurgency that employed a near complete repertoire of violent tactics in order to achieve an independent homeland. Further, the LTTE enjoyed massive support, financial and material, from fellow ethnics in India and Tamil communities in other parts of the world.

Despite thousands of deaths involving both Tamils and Sinhalese over the years, efforts to achieve a negotiated settlement failed. There was a "hurting stalemate" in the fighting—a precondition for a compromise settlement—at least for a while, but neither the Norwegians, who had no national interest in the outcome of the fighting, nor the Indians, who had some, were able to achieve a compromise settlement. One deadlock in the negotiations followed another until the Sri Lankan government and its Sinhalese supporters reached the conclusion that nothing short of complete independence would satisfy the LTTE, an outcome completely unacceptable to the government.[13] As a consequence of this conclusion the fighting was resumed and the LTTE was crushed and its intransigent leader killed exclusively through the use of military force.

Italian terrorism from the 1960s to the 1980s

Among the countries of Western Europe, Italy experienced the worst episode of terrorist violence during the decade and a half from 1968 to the early 1980s. The various terrorist organizations that appeared in these years were unusual in a number of respects, in addition to their sheer number. First, separatism was not a significant factor in bringing them to life. Unlike the situations in Northern Ireland and Spain (or to a lesser extent France over the status of Corsica) where the PIRA and ETA carried out attacks in order to achieve nationalist and separatist aims, no Italian groups emerged seeking independence for Sicily, Sardinia, Val d'Aosta etc. Second, Italian terrorism was driven to a large extent by political ideology, not nationalism. But unlike other West European democracies, where the major groups pursued the cause of left-wing revolution, Italy included several neo-fascist organizations whose goals were the destruction of the country's left-wing political parties and the imposition of a military dictatorship. A third way in which Italy differed from its democratic counterparts is the longer duration of its episode. Unlike Germany or West Germany, France, Japan, and the United States, countries where the "generation of '68" gave rise to a single wave of ideologically inspired terrorism that lasted for approximately half a decade, Italy experienced a second wave of terrorism, with a new collection of groups active from 1976 forward. Finally, the defeat of the groups involved in terrorism was achieved by the Italian police, without either a declaration of martial law or the intervention of the military. Italian democracy was certainly threatened but it did not give way: no martial law. We are not dealing with another Sri Lanka or Latin America for that matter.

There's an old saying that in the ex-Soviet Union nothing was said but that everything was understood while in Italy everything was said but nothing was understood. Italy's terrorists were nothing if not voluble. They had quite a bit to say for all those willing to listen to them or read their various commentaries. To compound the problem of comprehension, Italy is also the home of *dietroismo* (literally "behindism"), a view that behind every major political happening a conspiracy, involving a handful of powerful individuals, may be detected. Nothing or very little is as it appears to be on the surface. With these difficulties in mind let us attempt to disentangle fact from self-serving fiction and explain the political context from which Italian terrorism emerged at the end of the 1960s.

Italian politics had been dominated by the Christian Democratic Party (DC) from the end of World War II through the period with which we are concerned. All the country's prime ministers and a majority of cabinet members had been drawn from the DC. The party though did not command a majority of support among voters. This meant the DC had to find coalition partners with whom to ally in order to form governments. The DC's rule appeared to be permanent and indispensable because the second most popular party in the system were the Communists (PCI). Despite the fact the PCI depicted itself as unlike its counterparts in Europe in that it supported constitutional procedures rather than revolution, a large segment of the electorate was skeptical of this commitment. In effect, the Italian system was "blocked" or stalemated. To compound the problems with Italian democracy was the fact that at the right end of the ideological spectrum was an heir to Mussolini's tradition, a neo-fascist political party, the Italian Social Movement (MSI) whose leaders were radically anti-communist and who offered very limited support for democracy. Despite its anti-democratic reputation the MSI was widely understood to be a party dominated by aging "nostalgics," a minor annoyance rather than a serious contender for power. There were, however, radical elements within the MSI during the 1950s who decided to split off and found new "extra-parliamentary" organizations, the New Order (ON) and the National Vanguard (AN), whose outlook was far more radical.[14] Their then youthful leaders did not believe in parliamentary democracy and regarded political violence as a necessary means for achieving their authoritarian ends.

Against this background, Italy entered the 1960s, the era of the Vietnam War and of student protests throughout much of the Western world. The political environment in Italy underwent a process of radicalization. In 1967 and 1968 labor groups in the northern cities of Milan, Turin, and Genoa took to the streets to protest about wages and working conditions. At virtually the same time the PCI leadership adopted a conciliatory attitude towards the DC and the country's constitutional order in general. Enrico Berlinguer, the PCI leader, proposed an "historic compromise" whereby his party along with the DC and the Socialists would form a long-term coalition arrangement to run the country and restore stability. In effect, the PCI was determined to pursue a policy of deradicalization just as the Italian Left in general was becoming increasingly radicalized as talk of "revolution" began to fill the air.

Those filling the air with this revolutionary rhetoric belonged to the extra-parliamentary left. In the period 1967–1970 new groups with such names as The Struggle Continues, Worker Power, and Worker Vanguard emerged. They were largely student-led movements that sought to recruit a working-class clientele in plants and factories in Italy's major cities— particularly during the "hot autumn" of 1969 when labor contracts came up for renewal and when wildcat strikes became commonplace. In addition to these extra-parliamentary movements, groups with more openly violent orientations appeared—the Partisan Action Squads and the Red Brigades.

In what was rapidly becoming an incandescent atmosphere involving student protests and wildcat strikes, a bomb was detonated at the National Agricultural Bank in Milan on December 12, 1969. More than a dozen bank customers were killed by the blast. At first the police blamed the attack on left-wing revolutionaries and promptly arrested two anarchists. One of them, Giuseppe Pinelli, died as the result of a fall from the third story of Milan's police headquarters. The police claimed suicide, but journalists suspected otherwise.

Within a short time the story began to unravel. Witnesses began to come forward and disclose that the bombing was really the work of a neo-fascist band, acting in disguise, whose goal was to have the Italian public blame "reds" for the terrorism. In this way the public would eventually become conditioned for a seizure of power by elements within the police and military establishment, a coup as had occurred in Greece a few years earlier.

This tactic became known as the "strategy of tensions." MSI legis-lators, elements within the Defense Intelligence Agency (SID), and neo-fascists drawn from ON and AN committed themselves to simul-taneously demand a restoration of law and order while waging a terrorist campaign to achieve maximum disruption. And over the next half decade neo-fascist groups set off bombs at public places (e.g., Brescia) in the cities and along railroad tracks in order to derail passenger trains (e.g., traveling between Florence and Bologna) in the hope of killing as many travelers as possible.[15]

There was even an attempted coup d'etat. Prince Valerio Borghese, a World War II "hero" of the Fascist military, created a neo-fascist group, composed largely of Fascist veterans, the National Front (FN). And on the evening of December 7, 1970 its members gathered in front of the interior ministry and public television headquarters in Rome waiting for a signal to seize control of these key buildings. The signal never came and the FN militants dispersed. Prince Borghese then fled into exile in Spain.

By the mid-1970s it was clear that the "strategy of tensions" had failed. Leaders of both the ON and AN were tried for their terrorist violence and both organizations were placed "outside the law." The involvement of elements within SID in the neo-fascist scheme caused a scandal and set off a parliamentary investigation aimed at making the intelligence agency more accountable to democratic institutions. So for most intents and purposes the neo-fascist project to eliminate the Left and destroy Italian democracy had been brought to a successful conclusion.

The first wave of left-wing terrorism followed about the same trajectory as its neo-fascist counterpart. During this early phase, the "armed struggle" was dominated by three groups: the Partisan Action Group (GAP), the Nuclei of Armed Proletarians (NAP), and the BR.[16] GAP was the creation of Giangiacomo Feltrinelli, a multi-millionaire publisher and an admirer of Fidel Castro who conceived Italy in 1969 to be on the verge of a Fascist coup. To thwart the coup he sought to revive the spirit of the World War II era anti-fascist resistance movement. After a handful of attacks in Genoa, Feltrinelli managed to "decapitate" himself by falling off an electric power tower in Milan that he had intended to blow up. The NAP represented an amalgam of petty criminals who had been politicized by members of LC ("Lotta Continua," or "Continuous Struggle") while serving time in a Neapolitan prison. After their release these "Napisti" staged a series of bank robberies in Rome and a few northern cities. NAP's career ended shortly after its leader, a former Sicilian bandit, was shot dead by the police while reclining on the Spanish Steps in Rome.

The BR was a much more serious undertaking. It was the only group whose activities spanned the two waves of Italian terrorism. Its founders, members of its "historic nucleus," were drawn from three sources: students from the northern universities (especially the University of Trento), former Young Communists from "Red Belt" cities like Bologna, and young workers drawn from plants and factories in Milan and Turin (the FIAT Mirafiori plant in particular).

At first BR militants engaged in "armed propaganda" by burning the autos of corporate executives widely despised by the company's blue collar workforce. From there the BR began kidnapping the personnel directors of businesses whose practices it thought to be draconian. These bosses were then subject to proletarian trials and forced to wear dunce caps and confess their crimes against the working class, after which they were released. Yet by the end of 1973 the BR had not killed anyone; its attacks more attention-getting theatrics than violent.

The BR's turn towards violence came when it turned away from business targets and towards the Italian state and its personnel. In April 1974 the BR kidnapped a judge in Genoa, demanding the release of imprisoned terrorists in exchange for his freedom. The state prosecutor in the city agreed to the exchange but then reneged after the BR released the judge. It was in the aftermath of this event that the BR killed for the first time. In retaliation for a bombing at an anti-fascist rally in Brescia, Brigadisti entered the MSI headquarters in Padua and shot dead the two neo-fascists they found inside.

Following these cases the authorities reacted to the terrorism. The interior ministry created a special inspectorate whose purpose was to pursue and prosecute the terrorists, left and right. At the same time in Turin the Carabinieri (state police) set up a special anti-terrorism unit aimed specifically at the BR. Furthermore, the law was strengthened to enhance the sentences of those convicted of terrorism-related crimes and make membership in a neo-fascist band a crime in itself.

The results were not long in coming. By 1975 most members of the BR were in prison awaiting trial. The neo-fascists were more elusive, since they evidently enjoyed the protection of elements within Italy's intelligence and security apparatus. Nonetheless, the neo-fascist "strategy of tensions" had been uncovered and defeated. ON had been outlawed and various figures prosecuted for their crimes, e.g., placement of a bomb in front of an elementary school in Rome. Also, the DC-led government was pushing through parliament a comprehensive reform of the scandal-plagued SID, the intelligence agency.

By the mid-1970s Italian citizens then had good reason to believe the terrorist episode had come to an end. (Apparently so did the government because it dissolved the police unit it had created to fight the BR.) But Italian terrorism was hardly at an end. The violence underwent a dramatic revival in 1976 with the appearance of new groups and the revitalization of old ones.

The neo-fascists in effect changed their "war aims." Instead of seeking to topple the democratic regime and replace it with a fascist-style "strong state," they reached the conclusion that the Italian system was so corrupt as to be beyond redemption. Accordingly, they sought to attack or "disarticulate" it via a strategy of "armed spontaneity."[17] "We are not interested in seizing power, not even, per se, in establishing a new order

. . . what interests us is combat, action in itself, the daily struggle to assert our own nature."[18]

New terrorist groups emerged. Composed largely of disaffected MSI youth and older veterans of ON and AN largely from Rome and Milan, the Nuclei of Armed Revolutionaries (NAR), Third Position (TP), and Let's Build Action (Costruiamo l'Azione) launched a series of attacks over the next several years. Among other things, they staged bank robberies, stole weapons, carried out hit and run attacks on Rome's city hall and other public buildings, and assassinated various state officials. The most prominent of the latter was a Roman judge charged with the responsibility of investigating neo-fascist violence.

Far and away the most lethal neo-fascist attack in these years was the August 2, 1980 bombing of the waiting room at the Bologna railroad station. Carried out by members of NAR, the explosion killed eighty-five people and left hundreds injured. Until the more recent operations by groups from the Middle East, the Bologna bombing stood as the worst single terrorist attack in postwar Europe. Some of the perpetrators fled abroad and the initial reaction of the authorities to the crime was sluggish, to say the least (there were suspicions that a secretive Masonic lodge Propaganda Due was involved). Eventually though those responsible were prosecuted, found guilty, and given life sentences.

The situation on the revolutionary left was equally if not more complicated. A second generation of groups joined the conflict following Italy's 1976 parliamentary elections. This contest had resulted in the DC's return to power—much to the disgust of thousands of young people who had hoped for change and a PCI victory. One result of this development was the appearance of two significant terrorist groups, Front Line (PL) and Autonomy (Autonomia). As an organization PL followed the same hierarchical format as the BR. Autonomy, on the other hand, introduced the practice of "diffuse terrorism," decentralized organizationally and consisting largely of part-time militants.[19]

It was the BR, however, that posed the major threat to Italian democracy. In the period 1976–1977 it underwent a major revival. In 1976 a BR unit assassinated the Genoa prosecutor who had promised to release prisoners in exchange for the freedom of the kidnapped judge. Other figures, mostly DC politicians and state officials, were gunned down. And at the end of 1977 the BR carried out its most spectacular attack. Members of its Rome "column" kidnapped the former DC Prime Minister Aldo Moro.[20] Moro, a key figure in the country's postwar political life, was held captive for fifty-five days and then murdered after the government refused repeated demands that it release the BR's "historic nucleus" in exchange for Moro's liberation.

It was in the aftermath of the Moro case that the Italian government made a concerted effort to defeat the entire terrorist project. Parliament adopted a series of measures whose implementation proved decisive. A new crime was introduced on "Terrorism and Subversion of the Democratic Order." Rules governing search and seizure were relaxed. The length of time suspects could be held without access to an attorney was extended. Penalties were enhanced for those found guilty of terrorism-related crimes. Finally, and decisively, "emergency" legislation was enacted that offered the possibility of "disassociation" and "repentance." These measures provided that if an individual was willing to disassociate himself or herself from a terrorist group they would receive a reduced sentence for their crimes. This measure, in effect, permitted individuals to disclose information about the whereabouts of their former colleagues—some would say betray—in exchange for less time in prison. The law on "repentance" went further. If terrorists were willing to "come in from the cold" and tell the police all they knew about the group to which they had belonged, except in the case of murder, they would be able to be released after serving a short prison sentence.[21]

Reforms in Italy's police apparatus in the years immediately following the Moro case increased the likelihood of BR members and the members of the other revolutionary terrorist groups being captured. The chances of being arrested or shot by the police increased, so that the opportunity for a return to a normal life, via disassociation and repentance, became more appealing. These measures produced a cascade effect. A handful of terrorists would be arrested. They would then "disassociate" or "repent," which meant they identified the names and whereabouts of their erstwhile colleagues. The latter would be arrested and they, in turn, would repeat the process until hundreds of terrorists were arrested. The kidnapping by the BR of an American general James Dozier in 1980 and his subsequent liberation in 1981 by a special police unit accelerated this process, so that by 1982 Italy's "years of lead" had come to an end.

The defeat inflicted by the Italian state on the numerous terrorist groups that aimed to topple it was accomplished without military intervention or any other serious disruption of its constitutional democracy. The Italian system abounds with structural flaws as well as the personal failings of its "political class." Despite these weaknesses, the terrorist episode left few if any long-term effects.

Iran: vigilante justice and the Islamic Republic

Today when most observers think of the link between Iran and terrorism what comes to mind initially is the role that country has played in sponsoring or promoting terrorist violence abroad. This involvement has taken two forms. First, Tehran has provided assistance to the Lebanese group Hezbollah along with Shiite militia groups active in Iraq following the overthrow of Saddam Hussein by US forces in 2003. Before that a small Iranian-backed group, Hezbollah in Saudi Arabia, was responsible for the bombing of Khobar Towers, an apartment complex near Riyadh that killed more than a dozen American service personnel.[22] Second, the Iranian government has undertaken terrorist attacks itself. Exiled opponents of the regime have been murdered in Paris and elsewhere by agents sent by Tehran. The most spectacular of these transnational killings was the joint Tehran–Hezbollah operation in Buenos Aires in 1993. This bombing of the city's Jewish Community Center killed more than ninety people. In terms of state terrorism, Tehran has also used Basij militia men and its Revolutionary Guards to repress, apparently success-fully, the massive protests that followed the "re-election" of Mahmoud Ahmadinejad in 2009.

In view of this track record, it may be difficult to recall that the newly established Islamic Republic in Tehran was itself the target of a substantial wave of terrorism during the early 1980s. This episode occurred in the wake of the revolutionary upheaval of 1978–1979 that overthrew the Shah and led to the installation of a clerical regime headed by the Ayatollah Khomeini.[23]

In the few years between the Shah's flight into exile and the consolidation of clerical power it was by no means clear that Khomeini and his followers were destined to prevail. Other groups had participated in bringing about the monarchy's collapse, including the Communist Tudeh party. While Iranian communists made an effort to accommodate themselves to the new "anti-imperialist" forces in control of state institutions, others did not. Among the most important of these armed dissidents were the Marxist Fedayeen-e Khalq (Devotees of the People) and the Islamic Mojahedin-e Khalq (Fighters for the People). These groups, heavily composed of university students, regarded themselves as every bit as revolutionary as the revered Khomeini's followers.[24]

In order to prevent the consolidation of the Islamic Republic, whose constitution was approved by referendum in 1979, the Fedayeen and most importantly the Mojahedin launched a wave of terrorist attacks in the succeeding years. Accordingly, on June 28, 1981 the Mojahedin detonated a bomb in the building where a meeting of the ruling Islamic Republican Party (IRP) was under way. The explosion killed the IRP secretary general, four cabinet members, six undersecretaries, twenty-seven parliamentary deputies, among others. Two months later the Mojahedin set off another bomb at the prime minister's office. On this occasion the group managed to kill Iran's president and prime minister along with the head of the national police. In short, within a few months the Mojahedin had managed to eliminate most of the Islamic Republic's leadership.[25] Nor were these terrorists done with their campaign of assassination; over the balance of 1981 they murdered Khomeini-appointed prayer leaders in Tabriz, Shariz, and other cities. The prayer leaders served as conduits distributing Khomeini's instructions from Tehran to the rest of the country. The Mojahedin appeared to be in the process of dismantling the Islamic Republic's core leadership body by body.

The Mojahedin was not alone. In the same period, a time when Iran was under attack from Saddam Hussein's Iraq, the Fedayeen and other revolutionary groups launched their own campaigns against the shaken and evidently transitional authorities. Some militants went underground; others waged street battles against pro-Khomeini youth in Bandar Abbas, Abadan, Tabriz, and other cities. It was also at about this time that the Mojahedin chose the path of direct confrontation with the regime. In 1982 the Mojahedin leaders sent their cadres into the streets of Tehran and the other cities to wage a renewed revolutionary challenge to Khomeini's forces, the revolutionary guards in particular. This was no small effort. The Mojahedin claimed a membership of over ten thousand in Tehran alone: many were armed.[26] The leaders' objective was to overwhelm the Revolutionary Guard's capacity to respond.

The Mojahedin miscalculated, to put it mildly. As Walter Laqueur puts it:

> The terrorists had made a fatal mistake in their assessment of the political situation: for so many years they had claimed in their propaganda that the Shah was the cruelest despot in the world and the SAVAK, his secret police, was the most effective tool of repression, capable of committing any atrocity. In the end they came to believe their own propaganda. Yet, in actual fact, compared with Khomeini and his followers, the Shah was a moderate who was subject to many restraints, and SAVAK, despite its notoriety, was neither particularly effective nor as brutal as its successor.[27]

Within a few months the threat posed by the Mojahedin and the other groups came to an end. Its handful of surviving leaders wound up in Paris rather than Tehran. Khomeini's followers, the Revolutionary Guards, the revolutionary courts, and the new secret police reacted with great brutality, at least by Western standards. No due process, no *habeas corpus*, no probable cause. If they were lucky, Mojahedin were arrested and put in prison. Torture and the firing squad came later. More commonly the terrorists were subject to summary executions. Street demonstrations were repressed; even twelve- and thirteen-year-old children were executed. Parents of these and other children similarly killed often received their mutilated bodies some days later. Teachers were shot and killed in front of their pupils. Wounded Mojahedin were dragged out of hospitals and executed on the grounds these "evil-doers" were not entitled to medical treatment. "Executions of fifty a day became routine. Some 149 persons were executed on 19 September [1981] alone, 110 on a single day a week later."[28]

The authorities made little attempt to disguise these murders. Shaul Bakhash reports, for example, that in September 1981 two Mojahedin were publicly hanged from the arch of a widely used bridge—to discourage the others. In the months between June 1981 and September 1983 Amnesty International estimated that 2,946 people, a majority of whom were high school and college students, were meted out street-corner justice and executed in the ways just described. And so in this way the terrorist threat to Iran's new clerical regime came to an end. Brutal repression had worked.

Reasons for more terrorist defeats and the issue of "decapitation"

To this point we have examined three instances in which terrorist campaigns were successfully repressed. These were all cases in which the groups waging the campaigns seemed formidable. They had memberships numbering in the thousands and considerable resources at their disposal. None of them though managed to achieve their strategic objectives. They met their defeats in somewhat different ways. In the case of Sri Lanka it took a full military onslaught by the country's armed forces to achieve this result, after more than a decade of on and off negotiations. In Italy it was the police, notably the carabinieri, along with the reformed intelligence agencies, that managed to collapse the array of revolutionary groups, the BR most prominently, with which they were confronted. The Italian authorities had made the shrewd calculation that many left-wing terrorists would respond to the incentives offered by the laws on disassociation and repentance to "give up" their colleagues, replete with arms caches and hiding places. Iran essentially introduced a reign of terror as the principal means for defeating its opponents, using means not easily available to democratic countries concerned about domestic enemies.

Before proceeding to discuss cases where the end of terrorist groups was caused to a large extent by the decapitation of their leaders, we think it would make sense to consider instances where terrorist campaigns might have occurred but did not. These were situations where an array of "risk factors" existed pointing in the direction of an outbreak of terrorism but where no such outbreak occurred. The cases we have in mind involve the Soviet Union and the People's Republic of China. They may be described briefly.

During the 1920s an exiled White Russian community grew up in Harbin Manchuria. At one point the population reached over 150,000 members. Bitterly hostile to the Soviet regime, many of these White Russians became attracted to European Fascism and Nazism. The result was that by the mid-1930s there was an All-Russian Fascist Party operating along the border between the Japanese-controlled Manchuria and the Soviet Union committed to the destruction of the hated communist system.[29] To a limited extent, the Japanese provided state support for the initiative. The Russian Fascists sent saboteurs (i.e., terrorists) across the border into the USSR to assassinate communist officials and carry out sabotage operations. Nothing was ever heard from these Fascist infiltrators again. After the war, Stalin promised amnesty to the Russian Fascist leaders if they would simply admit their mistake and return to their homeland. Some did. They were arrested immediately and subsequently executed.

In 1989 China experienced the Tiananmen Square episode. Thousands of young people gathered at Tiananmen Square in Beijing to protest against Chinese government policies and to demand a more open democratic system. In Western Europe and the United States when similar mass protests were repressed by the authorities almost two decades earlier various small terrorist bands emerged as these protests subsided: the Weather Underground in the US and the June 2nd Movement in Germany may serve as examples. But nothing similar to this occurred in the People's Republic. Why not?

As in the case of the Russian Fascists the Chinese protestors faced an authoritarian regime that was willing to use the entire coercive apparatus of a modern state to prevent the emergence of insurgent campaigns by comparative handfuls of its opponents. "Risk factors" that in other national settings facilitated an outbreak of terrorist violence produced virtually none in the USSR and China.

"Decapitation" of its leadership is another widely discussed means by which a terrorist group may be defeated. By decapitation analysts have in mind either killing or arresting a group's key figures.[30] Aside from the fact "extra-judicial" killings pose legal and moral problems for the democracies, the issue is whether or not decapitation is effective in defeating terrorist bands. The tactic of "targeted killings" has been widely used by the Israelis in confronting Hamas, PIJ, the al-Aqsa

Martyrs' Brigades, and the more secular organizations it has confronted over the years. None of these groups has surrendered or disappeared. But we cannot help notice that the Al-Aqsa Intifada (2000–2004) has come to an end. The United States presently employs drone aircraft to fire Hellfire missiles (Hellfire seems an appropriate name for weapons launched against religious fanatics) in Afghanistan and Pakistan at Taliban and al-Qaeda targets.[31] And in some of Pakistan's major cities key figures in these groups have been arrested and held for trial. Yet in both countries the insurgencies persist. What is the evidence for the failure or success of "decapitation"?

Fortunately there is a recent study that offers a systematic analysis of the issue.[32] Using a variety of statistical routines Jenna Jordan evaluates the consequences of 298 cases of leadership decapitations from 1945 to 2004. She reports that the success or failure of the tactic is strongly related to a group's age, size, and type. Specifically, older, more established groups as well as larger ones are less likely to be collapsed by decapitation. The same generalization applies to the group's type or political orientation. Religious groups are less vulnerable to decapitation than groups inspired by ideological considerations, e.g., Marxism–Leninism. Overall, Jordan concludes decapitation is not an effective means for bringing about the end of a terrorist group's operations.

We should introduce a qualification at this point concerning the meaning of leadership. Jihadi groups in Western Europe, with or without a direct association with al-Qaeda's central leadership located presumably along the Afghan–Pakistan border, are typically led by what Petter Nesser refers to as "entrepreneurs."[33] These are individuals who recruit new members, galvanize the group, and plan new operations such as those carried out in Madrid in 2004, the commuter train bombings, and the underground suicide attacks in London the following year. To this list of entrepreneurs we should add the imams or prayer leaders at such radical mosques as Finsbury Park in London and the Islamic Cultural Center in Milan. The arrest or deportation of such radical prayer leaders and terrorist "entrepreneurs" as Abu Hamza in Great Britain, France, Italy, and other European countries in the years following these attacks may not have decapitated al-Qaeda as a whole, but it certainly brought an end to many jihadi cells planning additional attacks against the United States and its allies.

The Shining Path and the Supreme Truth

Two cases in which the decapitation of terrorist groups clearly brought about their defeat are the Sendero Luminoso (Shining Path) in Peru and

Aum Shinrikyo (Supreme Truth) in Japan. In both instances the leaders involved, Abimael Guzman and Shoko Asahara, respectively, were charismatic figures who elicited the obedience and even veneration of their followers. Sendero was a secular communist organization while Aum was a religious one.

Sendero grew out of a succession of splits within Peru's pro-Soviet communist party in the 1960s. Maoists broke away from the party to pursue a revolutionary policy against the authorities in Lima. One of the Maoists was a then young professor of philosophy at the University of Huamanga in the poverty-ridden and isolated province of Ayacucho in the Andes. Professor Guzman was largely responsible for transforming what was initially still another Latin American revolutionary or pseudo-revolutionary group of university students into a substantial armed force. After several trips to China during the years of the Cultural Revolution, Guzman committed himself to applying Mao's ideas to the Peruvian situation. He even developed his own version of Maoism to which his followers were supposed to adhere.

Initially based in Ayacucho the Sendero went through a gestation period, which included the formation of underground cells in other parts of the country, during the 1970s, until finally launching an armed struggle in 1980. Sendero announced its presence first by destroying ballots for the coming presidential elections and then by symbolically hanging dogs from lampposts in Lima, a gesture intended to show the fate of capitalism's "lapdogs." Sendero's armed struggle consisted of a mix of guerrilla strikes in Peru's highlands and urban terrorism at first with a particular focus on Peruvian officials. Guzman cited with approval Lenin's comment: "For the revolution to explode, it is not enough for those from below to not want to live as before. In addition there is a need for those from above to not be able to administer and govern as before."[34] The launching of this campaign coincided with the restoration of Peruvian democracy after more than a decade of military rule, a positive development to be sure but one that did little to alleviate the poverty of its native-American population.

Sendero's most spectacular early attack involved turning out the street lights in Lima, just as Pope John Paul II arrived in the city for an official visit in 1982; so that the Pontiff's motorcade had to make its way through the streets in darkness. There was less theatre and more blood-letting in subsequent conduct. Guzman (who came to call himself Presidente Gonzalo) and his followers killed close to 400 government officials, including mayors, between 1982 and 1989.[35] This number though pales in comparison to the overall number of people Sendero killed over the first ten years of its armed struggle.

Over the first ten years of the radical Maoist's people's war, more than twenty thousand Peruvians were killed, $10 billion worth of infrastructure was damaged or destroyed, some five hundred thousand internal refugees were generated, along with an almost equal number of emigrants, and there was a decline in gross domestic product of 30 percent and a cumulative inflation of more than two million percent. By 1990, such discouraging indicators suggested that a Shining Path victory was close at hand.[36]

At this time Sendero exercised effective control over five states that represented Peru's mountainous spine. The organization imposed a puritanical regimen wherever it ruled. Adulterers, alcoholics, and homosexuals were threatened and if they persisted were executed. Landowners were killed if they came to be regarded as mistreating their peasants, businessmen if they charged too high interest. In other words, Sendero imposed a "reign of terror and virtue" wherever they ruled.[37]

How was such a formidable group as Sendero defeated when it seemed as if it might actually achieve a strategic success? The answer is that a combination of factors brought about its collapse. David Scott Palmer points to a growing hubris within the organization that led it to make a series of significant mistakes, as well as a rethinking of its counter-insurgency strategy on the part of the government. Wherever it ruled or exercised power the local population came to hate Sendero more than they hated representatives of the government in Lima. In terms of the latter's policy for dealing with the insurgency, there was a new emphasis on winning the "hearts and minds" of the population. Finally, Guzman was captured in Lima in 1992 in the rear of a dance studio owned by a Sendero sympathizer. Presidente Gonzalo was then humiliated by his captors by being put on public display at an outdoor cell wearing an outlandish prison uniform. In the absence of their charismatic leader, Sendero suffered a precipitous decline in the rate of its violence and in its popularity among impoverished Peruvians. What began in tragedy ended in something approaching a farce.

For a time during the 1990s terrorism analysts regarded Japan's Aum Shinrikyo or the Supreme Truth as a major threat. The reason for this is that many observers believed that it had crossed a threshold. On March 20, 1995 members of Aum released sarin (nerve) gas from canisters in the Tokyo subway system in an attack that killed a dozen commuters and left a few thousand more injured. Aum had hoped to kill many more but the attack ran into technical problems so that a dozen was the best it could manage.[38] The Aum's leader had hoped to set off an end-of-the-world conflagration. What he did instead was draw attention to the likelihood that terrorists thereafter were going to employ weapons of mass destruction in order to achieve their increasingly chiliastic goals. Prior to Aum's attack observers tended to believe that terrorists "wanted a lot of people watching, not a lot of people dead." Now they came to believe, accurately enough, they also wanted a lot of people dead.

Aum Shinrikyo was a religious cult or "new religion" that was founded in Japan during the 1980s to draw adherents from the country's disenchanted young people. It represented one of several that emerged in these years to meet the spiritual longings of Japan's younger generation. At Aum's peak in the 1990s it drew some thousands of followers, including young scientists and engineers, who revered the group's charismatic founder and leader Shoko Asahara.[39] Asahara (whose real name was Matsumoto Chizuo) was a half-blind young man who began to claim special religious powers in 1985 after a series of misadventures. The same year he founded Aum he undertook a spiritual journey to India where he consulted Hindu and Buddhist scholars. Later he absorbed some of the ideas of Christianity as well, the Book of Revelation in particular. What resulted was a synthetic religion with Asahara as its seer and guide.

This visionary reached the conclusion that the end of the world was imminent and to hasten it along he committed himself and his worshipers to "forcing the end" by taking steps to set off Earth's apocalyptic conclusion. World War III was what he had in mind.

A cult of worship grew up around Master Asahara.[40] His followers came to revere him as a demigod. They even sold vials of his bath water because they believed it possessed special powers. Under Asahara's direction Aum established outposts in Moscow (it claimed thousands of members in Russia) and Western Australia. (The latter attracted the group's attention because of its deposits of uranium.) Unlike other crackpot cults—the People's Temple followers of the Rev. Jimmie Jones for example—Aum attracted scientifically minded young chemists, physicists, and engineers. Money did not seem all that hard to come by either. The group's scientific equipment came to rival that possessed by the laboratories of major Japanese universities.

To achieve Asahara's aims his followers began to experiment with lethal chemicals and various toxins. Neighbors complained of noxious smells coming from their offices. Several people died as a result of this experimentation. All these efforts culminated with the 1995 nerve gas attack in the Tokyo subway system.

Within a few months following the attack Japanese police arrested Master Asahara and his principal followers. They were tried and convicted for the murders. Aum's career in terrorism had come to an end as the result of its leader's apprehension. Aum persists but its remaining adherents vow to confine themselves to peaceful pursuits.[41]

Failure to recruit a new generation

Terrorist groups also suffer defeat when they are unable to recruit a new generation of members. As may be imagined, the attrition rate for members of such groups is high, as they are killed, arrested, or otherwise rendered *hors de combat*. In this regard we should consider the fate of the Weather Underground in the United States.

The Weathermen, as they were originally called, appeared in 1969–1970 as the massive student protest movement energized by the Vietnam War began to subside. During the 1960s the United States experienced what amounted to a massive generational rebellion, one that originated on the campuses of the University of California, Berkeley, and other major universities. Then, following the escalation of American participation in the Vietnam fighting in 1965–1966, it spread elsewhere to a younger generation of largely white middle-class youth impressed by the struggles of the civil rights movement with its emphasis on direct action.[42]

The anti-Vietnam protests of the mid-to-late 1960s gave rise to a variety of organizations inspired by Castro, Che Guevara, and Mao Tse-tung and other revolutionary figures. The most important of these groups was the Students for a Democratic Society (SDS) that helped initiate the era of the New Left with its Port Huron statement of 1962. As opposed to its "old left" predecessors the SDS emphasized the need for direct action in support of civil rights and opposition to nuclear proliferation. It also expressed disdain for capitalist greed as well as for the authoritarian politics of the Soviet Union and the conventional conduct of old-style communist parties.[43]

SDS chapters were created on college campuses throughout the United States. Their leaders promoted sit-ins, protests against military recruiters on campus and links between university research work and government institutions, the military especially. In some instances, San Francisco State for example, SDS and related groups managed to shut down the entire campus. Off-campus SDS organized marches and other types of direct action as well. As the Vietnam war came to be seen as "endless," the protests became increasingly violent as protesters "trashed" banks, stores, and other businesses they came to see as part of the establishment. The most spectacular of these demonstrations was staged at the 1968 Democratic Party national convention in Chicago.

As the "whole world was watching" on television thousands of anti-Vietnam protesters fought the Chicago police on the streets while the convention was under way. Hundreds were treated brutally by the police and many more were arrested. SDS organizers, the "Chicago Eight," were later tried for their role in what the court saw as a criminal conspiracy. It was in this context that the Weather Underground was born.

In the year following the Chicago Convention members of SDS staged what they described as "Days of Rage." SDS militants stormed through streets in Chicago vandalizing cars and smashing store windows in protest against the extension of the war and the FBI's crackdown on the area's Black Panther movement. This gesture proved to be a transition to covert violence and underground activity.

Following a 1970 meeting of its leadership in Flint Michigan about the best way of proceeding, the SDS formally dissolved itself. A crucial faction then embarked on a campaign of violence aimed at "bringing the war home." This faction became known at first as the Weathermen (named after a lyric in a Bob Dylan tune, "Ballad of a Thin Man") and later the Weather Underground. At first the attacks were public and aimed at persuading young people in general that the group was tough and serious.[44] They provoked fights with street gangs and invaded high schools encouraging the students to flee captivity.

Over the next half dozen years these revolutionaries carried out a series of bombings. These included attacks on the Department of Corrections in San Francisco and Sacramento, a precinct office of the New York Police Department, the National Guard headquarters at Kent State University, and offices at both Harvard and MIT. And following the 1973 anti-communist coup in Chile against Salvador Allende, the Weather Underground bombed the Oakland offices of the Anaconda Copper Corporation.

The most spectacular of these bombings was unintended. On March 6, 1970, members of the Weather Underground accidentally set off an explosion in a townhouse in Greenwich Village owned by the parents of one of the group's members (Cathy Wilkerson). Three people were killed but two survived the blast to fight another day. But to what end?

The Vietnam War ended. A new generation arose for whom the conflict had little meaning. None were recruited by or chose to join an organization whose members were on the run from the FBI. Members of the Weather Underground persisted in their revolutionary activities for a few more years. But by 1976 the organization had ceased to exist.

Loss of popularity

On some occasions groups turn to terrorism as a means of gaining support. In the Middle East, for example, Palestinian groups managed to enhance their levels of popular support by staging terrorist attacks on Israeli targets. Under the leadership of Yassir Arafat, Fatah and the PLO more generally became enormously popular in the years following the June 1967 Arab–Israeli war by virtue of these attacks. Later about the same may be said about the ascent of Hamas to a point where it was able to win open and democratic elections among Palestinian voters.[45] The strategy worked in the sense that small, often obscure extremist organizations used terrorism to trade their obscurity into worldwide prominence and political influence by depicting themselves as champions of an oppressed population.

More often than not the adoption of terrorism by extremist groups has no effect on their popular support, one way or another. As Martha Crenshaw notes, the causes that such groups typically advocate have little or no support in a national population and their leaders usually lack the patience required to mobilize such support.[46] During the 1970s Marxism had little support among workers or anyone else among West Germans, except for a minute subculture. But that did not inhibit the Red Army Faction or the June 2nd movement from waging terrorist campaigns on behalf of the ideology. About the same may be said about the Symbionese Liberation Army (SLA) in the United States. A group famous for its kidnapping of newspaper heiress Patty Hearst in 1973, the SLA began its career with virtually no support in the San Francisco Bay Area or the United States for that matter and ended it a few years later with no observable popular sympathy.

On some occasions though, the loss of popularity or the perceived loss of popular support has contributed to the defeat of terrorist organizations. In Uruguay the Tupamaros managed to achieve some level of popularity and a reputation as latter day Robin Hoods by stealing from the rich and giving to the poor. Members of the organization staged a robbery at a casino on the outskirts of Montevideo and subsequently distributed the proceeds to slum dwellers. However, when the Tupamaros assassinated a young police officer they suffered a decline in popular sympathy when the press called attention to the fact that the officer came from a humble background and that his widow was then left to raise their young children by herself.

Terrorist groups acting on behalf of a nationalist cause (see above) may achieve prominence and win support among their co-ethnics by attacking members of some enemy group, e.g., Israelis. However, when they stage terrorist attacks on members of their own national community, e.g., fellow Arabs, fellow Jordanians, that support may wane.

In recent years there has been a theological debate among Muslim advocates of jihad, including spokesmen for al-Qaeda, about the religious justification for killing other Muslims. The debate has involved the concept of *takfir*, the act by which some Muslims declare others to be apostates.[47] From the point of view of influential Sunni theologians, such a declaration may be applied to individuals, individual rulers (e.g., tyrants) for example, not collectivities. Hafez notes that most of the violence al-Qaeda-linked groups have inflicted since 9/11 have been committed against other Muslims, members of the Umma, or community of believers. Declaring whole communities, including women and children, to be renegades, violates basic principles of Islam.

What impact does an ensuing loss of popular support, real or perceived, have on the defeat of a terrorist group? In most cases the answer seems to be indirect. First, the slide in support may raise the likelihood that informants in the surrounding population will provide the authorities with valuable information. Second, potential new recruits will become increasingly reluctant to join an organization that becomes the target of ostracism by precisely the same segment in the population it claims to champion. Third, whether or not the decline in popular support is real or simply perceived, the authorities will feel less inhibited in using repressive means to bring about its defeat. Following the kidnapping and murder of Aldo Moro in 1978, the Italian authorities felt the BR had suffered a precipitous decline in support even among those Italians who favored radical change. This was evidently not the case, but the fact that the authorities believed it to be true led them to take steps they would have been reluctant to take if they did not. Then, there is the matter of terrorist group morale to consider.

Internal problems

The roles played by agents provocateur or police spies (as in the case of the Russian Social Democrats at the beginning of the twentieth century) in defeating terrorist groups are long-standing.[48] These are situations in which a government plants a spy (or recruits someone who's already a member) inside a terrorist group. Not only does the spy provide the authorities with crucial information about the group's plans but on occasion they may provoke the group to take on particularly risky operations or stage attacks intended by the provocateur to alienate its potential constituency. These agents may also take the initiative in sowing dissent within the group. The authorities may even benefit after the spy or provocateur's identity is disclosed. The group's members may become deeply suspicious of each others "real" commitments. And this type of group paranoia may make it especially wary of recruiting new members.

Not uncommonly members of terrorist groups develop a sense of their own importance. This is especially true for groups that manage to garner widespread publicity as the result of their operations. They assign key figures in the organization with important-sounding names: emir, foreign minister, telecommunications chief, etc. Often the group's spokesmen are transformed into terrorist celebrities. Thanks to the World Wide Web these groups are able to present themselves to audiences in ways unavailable in pre-Internet days. Often a gap develops between the group's view of themselves and the public's. What then?

If the public, particularly a group's self-defined constituency, reacts to its terrorism with indignation and public displays of opposition, e.g., protest marches, what happens to the group? For a while its internal dynamics are such that most members are able to shield themselves from external reality, but this reality cannot be kept out indefinitely.

When members become demoralized, what happens to the group? In most cases they rarely elect to dissolve it immediately. What happens, as Tore Bjørgo and John Horgan point out, is that the group begins to suffer individual defections. These defections take a variety of forms. In some instances members become disengaged psychologically and move from the center to the periphery of the group. In other cases disengagement may be physical in the sense that members flee the group and place as much distance between it and themselves as possible. Exit may also be accompanied by a process of deradicalization, a loss of faith in the group's ideas, though this need not be always the case.[49] In these cases the group may dribble away into insignificance.

Terrorist groups are almost by definition extremist in nature. But not all members of the organization need have the same outlook towards the use of violence. Some individuals regard violence as the only means by which the group can attain its objectives, reasoning that all other means have been tried and failed. Others, members that Cynthia Irvin labels "radicals," view the violence as necessary but are willing to consider other possibilities. Third, she identifies "politicos" members who are willing to negotiate an end to the violence in exchange for the group achieving some of its aims.[50]

If the authorities extend the possibility of a negotiated end to the conflict, the group, e.g., the IRA, is likely to fragment. The "politicos" especially will enter negotiations while the irreducible hardliners will assert betrayal and treason and, depending on the outcome of the negotiations, split off to form a new group, e.g., the Real IRA. The history of the Basque group ETA bears a resemblance to this pattern as well.

In Egypt there are two exceptionally violent groups that have undergone ideological or religious reorientations. In July 1997 the

Islamic Group, an organization responsible for the 1981 assassination of Anwar Sadat, declared a unilateral ceasefire against the Egyptian state. In 2007 the leadership of Al-Jihad, an almost equally violent group, also proclaimed an end to its terrorist campaign against the state.[51] It's true that many members of the two groups had been imprisoned by the Egyptian authorities but this is not the primary reason for their reorientation. In the case of the Islamic Group (IG), theologians from al-Azhar University in Cairo visited IG militants in prison and successfully persuaded them that their understanding of jihad and other Islamic concepts was incorrect. The militants also received religious literature that helped convince them of the veracity of the theologians' views. For al-Jihad it was the decision of a prominent cleric, Sayyed Imam al-Sherif, to abandon violence that made the difference. Imam al-Sherif, also one of the founders of al-Qaeda, wrote a book that was subsequently serialized in an Egyptian newspaper, in which he condemned attacks against the state as well as tourists and other innocents as fundamentally un-Islamic as well as counter-productive.[52]

These developments are of exceptional importance. Salafist jihadi groups, those linked to al-Qaeda especially, appear to be among the most fanatically committed to the terrorist path. The fact they have chosen to abandon it suggests similar groups in other countries may also be amenable to similar shifts in direction.

As we have sought to show in this chapter, terrorist groups typically fail to achieve their goals. Normally they are defeated as the result not of a single factor but a combination of the ways described above. We now intend to devote the next chapter to those occasions when terrorism has achieved success.

4 Success

When and how do terrorist groups succeed? And what is the meaning of success? Max Abrahams and other writers cited earlier in this commentary maintain that terrorism rarely works, if by "works" we mean that the groups carrying out the attacks achieve their self-professed goals. If the self-professed goal is something like worldwide revolution or the reestablishment of a caliphate throughout the entire House of Islam, failure is inherent in the task. It takes a substantial dose of self-deception to believe that a group equipped with a handful of pistols, AK-47s, or grenade launchers will be able to topple the political and religious order on a worldwide basis.

On the other hand, there are certainly analysts who believe that terrorism works. Alan Dershowitz, the well-known Harvard University law professor, makes such an argument.[1] Dershowitz refers specifically to the case of the Palestinians. He points out that the long list of terrorist attacks carried out by Palestinian groups both inside and outside the PLO umbrella during the 1970s and 1980s resulted in major benefits to the Palestinian cause including official recognition by the United Nations and many countries around the world, eventually including both the United States and Israel. Further, the use of terrorist tactics, the 1972 Munich Olympic massacre especially, raised the visibility of the Palestinians' plight to the worldwide stage. Roughly the same may be said in regard to Northern Ireland. In the absence of the paramilitary campaign waged by the PIRA would the British and Irish governments have pursued peace negotiations leading to the Good Friday Agreement? In these instances at least terrorism seems to have succeeded. But in what sense has it succeeded?

Israel still exists as an independent and largely Jewish state and Northern Ireland remains as part of the United Kingdom even though the PLO and PIRA have apparently ended their terrorist campaigns and undergone transformations into the Palestinian Authority and a peaceful political party, Sinn Fein. Have they then failed? It depends of course on how we choose to define success. If we mean by success in an armed conflict to mean something like "victory" in a modern war where the defeated party submits to the will and agrees to the aims of the victor, or in an internal war where the incumbent government is overthrown and insurgents seize control of state institutions as in the Russian civil war (1917–1920), then the answer has to be negative.[2]

But these organizations have not failed in the same way that the German Red Army Faction, the Italian Red Brigades, and the Weather Underground failed. In these instances small to mid-sized bands of modestly armed revolutionaries caused some casualties and did some material damage, but in the end most members were apprehended by the police and the groups themselves dissolved.

In the cases of the PLO and PIRA the results have been mixed. They achieved some of their aims but not others. It seems to us these partial successes may be divided into tactical and strategic achievements. When Dershowitz claims terrorism "works" he understands this to mean the PLO's terrorist attacks achieved a mixed result—publicity, popular sympathy, and official recognition as the "sole, legitimate voice of the Palestinian people." As yet however these results have not been translated into a separate Palestinian state, much less the elimination of Israel. Likewise, PIRA's violence promoted a power-sharing agreement (among other things) between Republicans and Unionists in Northern Ireland but not the separation of the province from the United Kingdom and its amalgamation with the Republic. Would these outcomes have been achieved in the absence of the violence?

There is another way in which the use of terrorism may succeed partially. We refer to tactical results. The judicious use of terrorism at the appropriate times may subvert peace negotiations between two warring parties. The decision by the Hamas leadership to launch a wave of suicide attacks on Israeli targets in 1994 was not accidental nor was Israeli Prime Minister Yitzhak Rabin's assassination by a right-wing Israeli law student an act of senseless violence. The perpetrators hoped their actions would undermine the Oslo peace accords (1993) between the PLO and the Israeli government. And as subsequent events have revealed, these terrorist attacks succeeded in polarizing or repolarizing the conflict.[3]

The same logic may be applied to the situation in Iraq in the years following the 2003 American invasion. Many of the bombings carried out by al-Qaeda in Mesopotamia and other violent Sunni organizations against Shiite holy sites, pilgrims, and Shiite neighborhoods in Baghdad and elsewhere were intended to prevent the peaceful development of a democratic government based on Sunni–Shiite–Kurdish cooperation and power-sharing. To this point the terrorist campaign has achieved, unlike the Israeli–Palestinian case, only a limited success.

There is also the use of terrorist violence as an auxiliary weapon in the arsenal of a broad-based insurgency. We sometimes forget that terrorism is a tactic that may be used by groups of varying sizes and different ambitions. Some groups have relied on it almost exclusively in their efforts to promote or prevent revolutions or cause or thwart the establishment of a new political entity. In other settings however the use of terrorism represents one form of violence along with guerrilla warfare tactics and violent mass protests in the repertoire of tactics of groups seeking to topple an incumbent regime.[4] Such violent tactics may be accompanied by political measures intended to achieve popular support for an insurgency in its pursuit of power.

For instance, it is widely believed that Fidel Castro's July 26 movement in Cuba made little or no use of terrorism in the course of its successful revolutionary campaign against the Batista dictatorship. This is not the case. Guerrilla warfare in conjunction with the regime's own corruption and ineptitude led to Batista's 1959 defeat, so the prevailing view has it. The record suggests though that terrorism did play a role, albeit a minor one, in Castro's operations. During 1958 the *New York Times* reported multiple acts of urban terrorism. Castro's followers detonated bombs all over Havana and parts of Eastern Cuba. And not only did they kidnap Argentine race-car driver Juan Fangio from his hotel room, they also kidnapped American civilians and US Navy personnel on more than one occasion. These attacks generated substantial publicity in both the American and Latin American press.[5]

The relevance of this discussion to the challenges currently facing the United States and its allies seem obvious. In Afghanistan and Pakistan the governments in Kabul and Islamabad confront not simply small terrorist groups but widespread insurgencies whose tactics include but are no means limited to terrorist attacks.

What is an insurgency? The current US military field manual describes an insurgency as

> an organized movement aimed at the overthrow of a constituted government through the use of subversion and armed conflict . . . Stated another way, [insurgency is] an organized protracted politico-military struggle designed to weaken the control and legitimacy of an established government, occupying power, or other political authority while increasing insurgent control.[6]

Bard O'Neill defines the concept as follows:

> Insurgency may be defined as a struggle between a non-ruling group
> and the ruling authorities in which the non-ruling group consciously
> uses political resources (e.g., organizational expertise, propaganda,
> and demonstrations) and violence to destroy, reformulate, or sustain
> the basis of legitimacy of one or more aspects of politics.[7]

We should note that both the field manual and O'Neill's definitions call
attention to the multiple tactics employed by members of insurgent
groups, typically a combination of political and military measures. Some
insurgencies may be smothered in the cradle as in Uruguay and Brazil
during the 1970s, but others may succeed in winning power as in China
in 1949 and Cuba a decade later. What role for terrorism in popular
insurgencies?

Mao Tse-tung divides the stages of a revolutionary insurgency or a
"protracted popular war" into three phases: strategic defensive, strategic
stalemate, and strategic offensive. At the first stage, when the state is
strong and the insurgency is weak, the revolutionaries confine themselves to low-level forms of violence as a means of making "agitation,
propaganda."[8] Acts of terrorism may be included during this initial phase
of operations, e.g., assassinations of mayors and other local officials,
bombs thrown into cafes and restaurants frequented by foreigners. Phases
two and three—assuming there are phases two and three—involve more
extensive types of violence including guerrilla hit-and-run attacks and
ultimately the use of conventional military means—as in 1975 at the end
of the Vietnam war.

There is no particular reason why insurgencies have to follow this
Maoist choreography. Some insurgents employ terrorism during the
middle and end of their efforts as well as their opening measures. This
would be true for the now failed Tamil insurgency in Sri Lanka where
the LTTE "Black Tigers" carried out terrorist attacks throughout the
conflict.

There is by now an extensive body of commentary on the sources or
"risk factors" making for the onset of insurgencies or internal wars.[9]
Some of these risk factors include a country's historical experience.
Countries, such as Colombia, with long-term experiences of resolving
their conflicts by violent means, are vulnerable to repeat performances.
Foreign invasion and occupation of a country also heightens its
susceptibility. A change in the ruling regime or repeated regime changes
may make for an insurgency directed against those in power, perhaps
on a temporary basis, in the national capital. Then there is Ted Gurr's

well-known formulation according to which people are prone to rebellion when their expectations for economic improvement exceed the reality even in the context of a growing economy.

By contrast to Gurr's viewpoint, there are those, such as Sidney Tarrow, who suggest that opposition movements coalesce based on the structure of available opportunity. "Movements are produced when political opportunities broaden, when they demonstrate the existence of allies and when they reveal the vulnerability of opponents."[10] An opposition movement is not necessarily an insurgency. Nevertheless, Tarrow calls our attention to the likelihood of a violent opposition emerging when the aggrieved become aware that there are opportunities to challenge the existing order because they become aware that those in power are vulnerable to attack.

It is certainly not a stand-alone factor, but insurgencies are clearly aided when there is a diaspora of fellow ethnics or nationals willing to provide material support. The Tamil Tigers were helped substantially by the willingness of Tamils in the Indian state of Tamil Nadu to provide resources as well as sanctuary to the LTTE. The same applies to external support offered to foreign states, typically ones whose territory is adjacent to the one that is the site of the insurgency. For example, the support provided by the Soviet Union to Mao's communist insurgency facilitated the success of the Chinese Revolution in 1949. Naturally rulers of the donor state will have their own reasons for aiding an insurgent movement. In the case of Afghanistan under Soviet control (1979–1988), Pakistan, Saudi Arabia, and the United States all had their own religious and strategic reasons for seeking to undermine the communist regime in Kabul by supporting the jihad of Muslim "holy warriors."

How do insurgencies or internal wars end? (We should not forget that an internal war may have more than one insurgent movement that may act either in concert or in conflict with one another.) In the early 1960s George Modelski specified a set of categories that still make sense to us.[11] According to Modelski, internal wars produce the following outcomes:

- incumbents win;
- challengers win;
- separation;
- settlement.

The first two outcomes require little explanation except to say that by Modelski's calculations internal wars are usually fights to the finish, unlike traditional international wars whose contestants have limited objectives. Less common, for Modelski, are outcomes where challengers and incumbents agree on a separation or partition. A separation outcome is one that results in the creation of a new state. Separation may mean national independence or secession. National independence is often achieved when a colonial power relinquishes control over a possession, as when the Philippines became independent from the United States following World War II. Secession occurs when what had been one state becomes two or more. At the end of the cold war what had been Czechoslovakia divided itself in two, the Czech Republic and Slovakia, after leaders in Bratislava demanded the creation of a separate country. For Modelski a settlement is achieved when the parties waging an internal war manage to achieve a compromise agreement in which challengers and incumbents get part of what they want while, at the same time, retaining their own identities.

In order to achieve either a separation or settlement result negotiations are required either between the parties in conflict acting by themselves or with the participation of an outside party. These days it is common for the United Nations or one of the regional organizations, e.g., the Organization of American States, Organization of African Unity, or one of Scandinavian countries to play such a role. According to William Zartman and other observers, a precondition for a successful negotiated outcome is a "hurting stalemate." The warring parties need reach the conclusion that the status quo will not permit them to reach their own aims and that the continuation of the fighting will do them more harm than good. Mutual pain leads to the parties' willingness to negotiate an end to the internal war.[12]

Recently two analysts from the Rand Corporation, Ben Connable and Martin Libicki, have made an effort to calculate how internal wars or insurgencies end. For the most part they adopt Modelski's categories (they combine "separation" and "settlement" into one category of "mixed" outcomes) and then compile an impressive body of data to explain how and why the various ends come about.[13] There are a host of factors that contribute to the success or failure of insurgencies. Our concern though is with the impact of terrorism on the end of insurgencies.

We should bear in mind that not all insurgent movements employ terrorism. Che Guevara's defeat in Bolivia likewise had little to do with the absence of terrorist attacks by his band. On the other hand we should not ignore the fact that incumbent regimes and their supporters may make extensive use of terrorism to defeat their challengers.[14] Often labeled as "human rights violations," during the 1980s authoritarian governments in Guatemala and El Salvador used terrorist attacks on civilians (e.g., priests and nuns) to defeat insurgents even though the latter made little use of this tactic themselves.

Does the use of terrorism help or hurt an insurgency's chances of success?

Connable and Libicki investigate the results of eighty-nine insurgencies ranging over the second half of the twentieth and first decade of the twenty-first centuries. In terms of their outcomes they report twenty-eight victories for the government and twenty-six for the insurgents. We take this almost coin-toss result to mean that insurgents stand a strong chance of winning their struggles despite the incumbents' normal material advantages. Nineteen conflicts produced mixed results (see p. 78) and sixteen remained unresolved as of 2007.[15]

Of the eighty-eight insurgencies included in the analysis only seventeen involved little or no use of terrorism (Table 4.1). In numerical terms then terrorist tactics, meaning attacks on civilian targets, represent a normal means by which modern insurgents do business. But does it seem to help or hurt their business?

The answer is that it depends on how terrorism is used. Not employing terrorism seems to have virtually no impact on the result. Attacking civilians or noncombatants does not harm or help an insurgency's long-run prospects. The outcome is the same in situations where both an insurgency and the government (or occupying force) the former seeks to topple, carry out terrorist attacks on civilians. Mutual brutality has little impact except on its victims.

Terrorism helps when it is used in a discriminating way. The chances of an insurgent win are improved significantly when the insurgents carry out targeted attacks, e.g., murders, kidnappings, on particular individuals or facilities. These attacks may win popular support when the targets involved are despised individuals or hated institutions. They may also weaken the ability of the incumbents to perform the normal functions of government if the targets are key officials.

The indiscriminate use of terrorism has a negative impact on an insurgency's success. Groups that attack civilian populations in hopes

Table 4.1 Number of insurgencies by insurgent use of terror

Outcome	Indiscriminate	Mutual atrocities	Discrete	Little or none
Government wins	11	3	8	4
Mixed outcome	5	3	6	4
Government loses	5	2	14	4
Ongoing	7	4	3	1

Source: Ben Connable and Martin Libicki, *How Insurgencies End* (Santa Monica, CA: Rand Corporation, 2010), p. 109.

of killing as many people as possible are more likely to lose in terms of achieving their ultimate aims. Suicide bombings of civilian targets have well-known advantages. For those that send the suicide bombers on their way, the attacks are far more likely to kill large numbers of people than other types of terrorist violence. This benefit and others appear indisputable. Those groups that send suicide bombers on their way, whether on foot on in vehicles, apparently believe the tactic is effective. Otherwise why would they persist in using it, as is presently the case in Iraq, Pakistan, and Afghanistan?

A number of answers come to mind. Most of them concern the satisfaction of the perpetrators' emotional and spiritual needs. Revenge: giving the enemy a dose of its own medicine. Religious: carrying out the will of the Divine by striking down nonbelievers or apostates or rival ethnics. The answer that we intend to explore in greater detail below concerns the tactical advantages of killing noncombatants indiscriminately.

There is a tendency in the West at least to regard terrorists as not only blood-thirsty but exceptionally clever and patient as well. This need not be the case. Byman and Fair report the following:

> Nowhere is the gap between sinister stereotype and ridiculous reality more apparent than in Afghanistan, where it is fair to say that the Taliban employ the world's worst suicide bombers: one in two manages to kill only himself. And this success rate hasn't improved at all in the five years they've been using suicide bombers, despite the experience of hundreds of attacks—or attempted attacks. In Afghanistan, as in many cultures, a manly embrace is a time-honored tradition for warriors before they go off to face death. Thus, many suicide bombers never make it out of their training camp or safe house, as the pressure from these group hugs triggers the explosives in suicide vests. According to several sources at the United Nations, as many as six would-be suicide bombers died last July after one such embrace in Pallkh.[16]

The point that we should make is that terrorist decision-makers need not recognize the often counterproductive result of killing on an indiscriminate basis—at least so far as the group's achievement of its long-term goals.

Tactical success

Lebanon provides us with at least two cases when terrorism achieved tactical successes for those engaged in this type of violence. The context for these tactical achievements was the Lebanese civil war that broke out in 1975 and did not end until the Saudi-brokered peace agreement in 1988. The contestants in this conflict included militias representing all the country's sectarian groups: Maronite Christian, Sunni Muslim, Shiite Muslim, and Druze. We should add to this mix the fact that Lebanon then as now served as host to large numbers of Palestinian refugees typically housed in camps supported by the UN Relief and Works Agency (UNRWA). Following the PLO's expulsion from Jordan in 1970, its major components relocated to Lebanon where they established offices in Beirut and paramilitary camps in the southern part of the country from which to stage attacks inside Israel. The latter was a concerned onlooker principally because Fatah, PFLP, and other PLO-related groups repeatedly staged terrorist attacks on Israeli civilians living in northern Israel. Syria was another player in Lebanese developments. Hafez al-Asad and other members of the Syrian ruling elite regarded all of Lebanon as rightfully part of their own country. Their principal opponents in this regard were the Western-oriented Maronite Christians organized under the banner of the Phalange Party. At any rate the Syrian security agency had a long history of intervening in domestic Lebanese politics.[17]

The outbreak of the civil war was triggered by a violent confrontation between Christian Phalangists and the Fatah fighters in Beirut. The conflict quickly deteriorated into a war of all against all as the fight spread throughout the country, with the Maronites seeking to retain their long-held political dominance and with the PLO groups siding with the Sunni militias. Chaos not only reigned but ruled as the ability of the government to maintain order largely evaporated.

In 1982 the Israelis invaded the southern part of Lebanon. This area had become known as "Fatahland" because of the supremacy the gun-wielding Palestinian groups had come to exercise over the local, largely Shiite population. The Begin government in Jerusalem used the pretext of an assassination attempt against the Israeli ambassador in London by members of the Abu Nidal organization to justify the invasion. In fact, following its peace treaty with Egypt, the Israelis saw an opportunity to remove the threat to the country's northern border posed by the Palestinian terrorist groups.

Instead of stopping their advance in southern Lebanon, Israeli forces marched all the way to the outskirts of Beirut. There they paused and demanded the removal of the PLO headquarters from the city. It was at this point that the United States, France, and other interested parties intervened and sought to put an end to the fighting. The American ambassador negotiated an agreement whereby the PLO would leave the country, and Syrian forces, which had been occupying part of the country, nominally as peacekeepers, also agreed to withdraw. In exchange for the agreement the United States guaranteed it would protect the Palestinian population from assault by the Phalange militia and the Israelis. Accordingly, as part of the agreement a Multinational Force (MNF) consisting of US, French, and Italian troops were deployed in and around Beirut to maintain order.[18] But with the PLO's departure for Tunisia, the MNF was withdrawn.

Following its withdrawal, Lebanese elections resulted in the election of Bachir Gemayel, a Maronite, to the presidency. Then in September 1982 Gemayel along with members of his entourage, was assassinated. As later investigations revealed it was the Syrians who were behind the killings, but in the heat of the moment Gemayel's followers blamed the Palestinians.

What followed were massacres at Palestinian refugee camps, Sabra and Chatila, carried out by Maronite gangs with ties to the Phalange. Israeli forces looked the other way as the massacres were carried out and as a result bear some of the responsibility for the killings.

These events created an international outcry. And as a result of them the MNF returned to Lebanon in order to protect the civilian population in Beirut and to strengthen the Lebanese government and military so that they could restore order. Unfortunately, the Lebanese government and military was widely perceived not as neutral but as in the hands of Christian elements. This meant they were viewed by the various Lebanese militias as simply other parties to the ongoing civil war. And so by seeking to strengthen them the Reagan administration was seen as taking the side of the Christians against the various Muslim and Druze contestants.

We need to consider another player in the Lebanese conflict. The Iranian Revolution of 1979–1980 served to radicalize Lebanon's large Shiite population, a population that despite its size was often at the bottom of the economic and political order. Centered in the southern and eastern (the Bekaa Valley) parts of the country along with the slums of south Beirut, the Shiites found inspiration in the achievements of the Ayatollah Khomeini and his followers in deposing the Shah and establishing an Islamic Republic.[19]

The first post-revolutionary manifestation of Shiite militancy was Amal (Hope), a political organization and militia that dominated Shia political life until the rise of Hezbollah (Party of God) in 1982. It was in the period during Hezbollah's formative years that terrorism was used to achieve its first major tactical success. A shadowy group calling itself Islamic Jihad was responsible for the suicide bombing of the American and French Embassies on April 18, 1983, explosions that caused major casualties (sixty-three dead at the US Embassy alone). Later, on October 23, 1983 a suicide bomber drove his truck into the US Marine Corp's compound near Beirut international airport. The ensuing explosion caused the death of 283 Marines. French forces were also targeted by another suicide bomber. The death toll in this case was fifty-eight. Why had these attacks happened and who was responsible?

The answer to the "why" question is that the United States and its French ally had been drawn into the Lebanese civil war on the side of the Christian-dominated government. American forces in particular had bombarded Druze and Shiite positions in the Shouf Mountains and elsewhere had engaged in fire-fights with their militia groups.[20]

The attacks were carried out by young Shiites trained and inspired by Iranian revolutionary guards sent to the Bekaa Valley by the revolutionary regime in Tehran. The Syrians (occupying Bekaa) played a significant role in supporting the bombings, obviously for their own advantage as a major player in Lebanese political life.

The tactical benefits were not long in coming. In February 1984 President Reagan ordered American forces from Lebanon and the French followed suit. Terrorism had achieved a tactical success for the newly emerged Hezbollah and for the Syrians.

In the years following these events the Israelis staged a series of phased withdraws from Lebanese territory. The Israeli withdrawal was promoted by a series of more than three dozen suicide bombings staged by Hezbollah, Amal "holy warriors" and various secular groups. The most spectacular of these attacks occurred in late 1982 when a Hezbollah suicide bomber drove a truck into Israeli military and intelligence headquarters in Tyre killing close to a hundred Israelis and their Arab prisoners.[21]

By 1985 these attacks plus other problems resulted in Israel's decision to retreat to a "security zone" in the southern part of Lebanon. Israeli forces in conjunction with the proxy Southern Lebanese Army (SLA) remained in this ten-mile-wide zone for the following fifteen years, until the decision by Ehud Barak's government's to completely withdraw from all of Lebanon.

The fight between Israel and Hezbollah was not confined to the "security zone." In 1992 the IDF assassinated Hezbollah leader Abbas Musawi (an individual who played a role in the Beirut bombings) along with members of his family. Several days later, in retaliation, Iranian agents, acting in conjunction with Hezbollah, executed a suicide attack in Buenos Aires. A truck bomb was used to attack the Israeli embassy killing twenty-nine people.[22] This was not the last event of its kind.

In 1994 and in reaction against continued Israeli occupation of Lebanese territory, Hezbollah operatives again acting in conjunction with Iran detonated another bomb in Buenos Aires. This time the target was the city's Jewish community center, resulting in eighty-six fatalities.

Over the next several years Hezbollah engaged in an armed conflict with Israeli and SLA forces in and around the "security zone." The conflict included the launching of Katyusha rockets by Hezbollah at targets in northern Israel. It also included ambushes of IDF and SLA patrols inside the "security zone." The consequence of all this fighting, terrorism, and guerrilla assaults was Israel's retreat from all of Lebanon.

In the case of Lebanon, terrorism helped Hezbollah and its allies to win two tactical victories. First, the United States and France withdrew their forces from Beirut in the face of multiple suicide bombings. Second, although the situation was more complicated, the Israeli decision to withdraw from part and eventually all of Lebanon was caused in part by the use of terrorist attacks by Hezbollah and Amal, with the support of the Islamic Republic in Iran.

Strategic success

There may be a few cases where terrorism was important though probably not vital to the strategic success of an insurgency. Britain's departure from Cyprus in 1959 was certainly accelerated by the efforts of Colonel George Grivas and his EOKA (National Organization of Cypriot Fighters) organization. By attacking British civilian and military targets Grivas and his followers scored a strategic success, though a partial one. EOKA was unable to achieve Enosis, a union between Greece and Cyprus, its ultimate aim.

About the same may be said in regard to the South Tyrol. This German-speaking area in the Dolomite Mountains had been given to Italy as part of the World War I peace settlement. Following World War II the area was merged with the largely Italian-speaking province of Trent (Trentino) to form the region of Trentino-Alto Adige. Spokesmen for the German-speaking population objected on the grounds that their culture and political influence was diluted by the merger. A South Tyrol People's Party emerged to demand autonomy. In Innsbruck, Austria, a small-scale insurgency was launched to detach the South Tyrol from Italy and reunite it with Austria. In the mid-1950s the Bergisel Bund staged a series of cross-border terrorist attacks on Italian targets. The result was a series of discussions between Austrian and Italian officials leading to the extension of a special grant of provincial autonomy for the German-speakers within the Italian republic, a partial victory in which terrorism played a modest role. International atmospherics were propitious for the insurgent successes.

The use of terrorism is rarely mentioned in connection with the postwar struggle over Vietnam. Most accounts of this struggle emphasize guerrilla warfare as the tactic employed by the insurgents against the French and American defenders of their local allies. These perceptions are certainly reinforced by films and television documentaries showing camouflaged insurgents attacking their enemies in dense rainforests and remote hilltops. Reality was somewhat different, however.

In the period between the end of World War II and the fall of Saigon to North Vietnamese forces in 1975 there were two separable conflicts. The first was a struggle between the Viet Minh, insurgents headed by Ho Chi Minh and Vo Nguyen Giap, and the French colonial power. This struggle ended with the 1954 Geneva peace conference and, as it turned out, the temporary division of the country into North and South Vietnam. After a not completely peaceful interval, a second struggle was launched by the Viet Cong and their allies in North Vietnam to bring about the country's unification under largely communist auspices. This war drew the massive involvement of American forces in 1966–1974 and culminated with the departure of the Americans following a Paris peace conference and the collapse of the South Vietnamese armed forces in 1975.[23]

With the exception of Graham Greene's novel *The Quiet American*, a book that focuses on the efforts of an American CIA agent (apparently a fictional depiction of a real person, Colonel Edward Lansdale) to establish a "third force" between the French and the Viet Minh, little seems to have been written about the place of terrorism in the fighting over Southeast Asia. But consider Stanley Karnow's description of this event near Saigon in 1946:

> At dawn Binh Xuyen terrorists led by Viet Minh agents slipped past . . . soldiers supposedly guarding the district. Smashing doors and windows, they broke into bedrooms and massacred one hundred fifty French and Eurasian civilians, sparing neither women nor children. They dragged a hundred more away as hostages, mutilating many more before freeing them later.[24]

This type of terrorist attack was hardly the last in the Viet Minh's effort to coerce the departure of the French.

The ensuing struggle did not follow the Maoist script either, which, we should recall, involves a stage in the fighting dominated by guerrilla warfare, a stage when the insurgents achieve something approaching parity with the incumbents. Along with guerrilla attacks, General Giap was able to mount a series of set-piece battles far earlier in the struggle than the Mao script would have called for.[25] These division-strength battles were made possible by the fact that after their 1949 victory the Chinese communists were willing to supply weapons and, if needed, sanctuary as well. The Viet Minh were able to recruit a sizable force early in the conflict, while the French, operating out of Hanoi, suffered from a number of serious limitations, both material and in terms of morale. French rule had lost its legitimacy, its right to rule, by virtue of the fact Vietnam had been occupied by the Japanese during the war. For many Vietnamese the French no longer represented an invulnerable presence. France's long-time puppet was the Emperor Bao Dai, a playboy ruler who spent much of the conflict on the French Riviera. With the reluctant consent of the United States, the French sent their armed forces, which often consisted of Moroccan recruits along with Legionnaires, from the Metropolis to Southeast Asia. This was at a time when France itself was struggling to recover from the effects of the German occupation and the ensuing devastation.

In the context of the cold war, particularly the success of Mao's revolution in China and North Korea's attack on South Korea in 1950, the United States was willing to provide the French with substantial material support, but the Eisenhower administration was unwilling to commit American ground forces to the struggle.

The French suffered a humiliating defeat in the spring of 1954 at Dien Bien Phu.[26] A peace conference in Geneva followed a few months later. In addition to the Viet Minh and the French the participants included the Chinese and, as observers, the Americans. The result of these negotiations was an interim peace agreement that provided for independence for North Vietnam, a Viet Minh stronghold, and an interim regime in the South, with national elections over the question of reunification to be held within two years. Ho and the Viet Minh had achieved a partial victory.

What place for terrorism in the struggle? The general answer is that terrorist attacks carried out by the Viet Minh (VM) played a subsidiary role in damaging the French war effort. The terrorism took two forms: the first carried out in the cities, the second in the countryside. In the major cities, bars, restaurants, cafes, cinemas, brothels, and other off-duty locales for French troops were bombed, often by VM agents throwing the bombs from passing motorcycles. In addition to killing French soldiers the terrorism damaged morale by leaving the impression there was no safe place for them to recover from the stresses of combat.[27] At least in Saigon the French and their Vietnamese allies managed to defeat the urban violence. They were much less successful in the countryside, however. On plantations and in villages the VM were able to assassinate French settlers and Vietnamese figures they identified as collaborators on a massive scale for the duration of the fighting. This statement captures the dynamic:

> As in all such wars, the French colonists were particularly vulnerable to attack by the VM, and the military had to protect them as best it could. The villages were rarely garrisoned, which meant that any headman who was friendly to the French could expect reprisals from the VM at some point. It was in any village's interest to be neutral at best, which in turn gave an impression of civilian collaboration with the VM to the French military—this led to French raids on villages to search out caches and VM troops, which raised civilian hostility to the French.[28]

In other words, the French forces did the VM's work for them. By reacting or overreacting to acts of terrorism at the village level the French helped their enemy to gain popular support among the local population. This counter-productive dynamic has repeated itself in various counter-insurgency operations in which the United States has engaged in subsequent decades, most recently in Afghanistan.[29]

In the years following France's departure from Southeast Asia, neutral governments were established in Cambodia and Laos. A communist regime was formed in North Vietnam under the leadership of Ho Chi Minh. In the South, however, the Geneva agreement's call for elections to determine national unification was not held. Ngo Dinh Diem, a former minister in the Emperor Bao Dai's cabinet, and other anti-communists sought to maintain an independent regime in South Vietnam while ignoring the stipulation for reunification elections. Ho and the Vietnamese communist leadership felt cheated by this result. At Geneva they had only agreed to this interim arrangement at the urging of the Chinese foreign minister Cho En-Lai. In the absence of elections the North became committed to altering what was becoming the status quo by fomenting insurrection in the South.

The Communists had in fact prepared for this contingency by leaving some thousands of their cadres behind in South Vietnam. As Walter Laqueur reports, the Viet Cong had already used terrorism effectively during the earlier conflict, and were prepared to do the same in the ensuing struggle:

> This is not to say that the Viet Cong behaved like the early Christian martyrs. They had already engaged in individual terrorism

on a massive scale in the first phase of the fighting (1949–1954). Systematic assassination of village leaders, local teachers and other 'dangerous elements' played a more important role in Vietnam than other Asian guerrilla wars.[30]

The North insisted that this renewed insurgency in the South involving a popular front movement the Viet Cong (VC) was entirely spontaneous and autonomous. But this was hardly the case. According to the Kennedy administration's estimate, by 1961 the VC had assassinated approximately 4,000 of these village notables.

Jeffrey Race, then an American officer, reported on VC activity in Long An province at the beginning of the 1960s. He describes the campaign directed against local officials:

> Beginning at the end of 1959 . . . in Long An many local officials resigned or ceased working because of the increased virulence of the warnings sent to them . . . Many suspected that something bad was coming, and their fears were realized during the week of Tet (January 18–25, 1960), the Vietnamese Lunar New year, in a series of armed actions which created a profound and lasting psychological impact in Long An.[31]

Race goes on to describe the VC killing of twenty-six people in this week-long period; the murders included hamlet and village leaders and youth leaders. The purpose:

> The Vietcong use terrorism to instill fear. In a hamlet they will pick out a couple of people who they say cooperate with the Americans and shoot them, to set an example . . . After they kill a few people, the whole hamlet is afraid and the Viet Cong can force them to cooperate.[32]

It was also by this time that the VC's growing guerrilla operations began to pose a serious threat to the Diem regime. The latter came to be dominated by members of his Catholic family in a predominantly Buddhist country. Allegations of discrimination by the Buddhist clergy led to public demonstrations in Saigon and, eventually, to acts of self-immolation; priests pouring gasoline over themselves and lighting themselves on fire in front of a crowd including Western reporters and television cameras.[33] To make matters worse the Diem government was notoriously corrupt and inept in dealing with the growing Viet Cong insurgency.

In October 1963 Diem was the target of a military coup d'etat. He was killed and replaced by General Duong Van Minh, one of the coup plotters. "Big" Minh and the succession of South Vietnamese military leaders who followed him proved somewhat better than the Diem family in fighting the Viet Cong and the North Vietnamese, but not enough to turn the tide in the conflict over the following years. Because of this, the Johnson administration made the strategic decision to intervene on a massive scale. Following the 1964 presidential elections, Johnson, despite some hesitation, decided to make a major commitment to the defense of South Vietnam, fearing that in the absence of this commitment the country would fall into the hands of the communist north and that eventually all of Southeast Asia would follow suit. So, beginning in 1965 hundreds of thousands of American military forces were committed to the struggle.

What place for terrorism in this conflict? Western media have tended to pay special attention to atrocities committed by members of the South Vietnamese and American military against peaceful villagers and other civilian bystanders. The March 1968 My Lai massacre, in which hundreds of villagers were killed by an American army patrol, drew special attention. We should not condone such war crimes but we should remind ourselves that, as Walter Laqueur remarked, the Viet Cong did not behave like the early Christian martyrs during these years.

In the period between 1960 and 1965 the US Mission in Saigon estimated that Viet Cong killed over 9,000 Vietnamese civilians as the pace of the insurgency picked up. Some examples should suffice at least to capture the milieu:

> 23 August 1960: Two school teachers . . . are preparing lessons at home when communists arrive and force them at gun point to go to their school . . . in Phong Dinh province. There they find two men tied to the school veranda. The communists read the death order of the two men, named Canh and Van. They are executed, presumably to intimidate the school teachers.

> 28 September 1960: Father Hoang Ngoc Minh . . . priest of Kontum parish, is riding from Tan Canh to Kondela. A communist road block halts his car. A bullet smashes into him. The guerrillas drive bamboo spears into Father Minh's body, then one fires a submachine gun point blank killing him. The driver . . . his nephew, is seriously wounded.

> 6 December 1960: Terrorists dynamite the kitchen at the Saigon Golf Club, killing a Vietnamese kitchen helper and injuring two Vietnamese cooks.

22 March 1961: A truck carrying 20 girls is dynamited on the Saigon-Vung Tau road. The girls are returning from Saigon where they have taken part in a Trung Sisters Day celebration. After the explosion terrorists open fire on the survivors. Two of the girls are killed and ten wounded. The girls are unarmed and traveling without escort.

16 February 1964: Three Americans are killed and 32 injured, most of them US dependents, when terrorists bomb the Kinh Do movie theatre in Saigon.[34]

From 1966 forward the Public Safety Division of the US Mission in Saigon compiled statistics about terrorist attacks carried out by the Viet Cong against civilian targets in the midst of their war with the South Vietnamese and American armed forces. The more conventional modes of fighting tended to obscure the terrorism. Despite their obscurity, the numbers of Viet Cong terrorist attacks is impressive, particularly if we limit ourselves to the most serious types of terrorism.

The figures recorded in Table 4.2 suggest that the volume of Viet Cong terrorism in this three year period, 1966–1969, rivals those of the most lethal terrorist campaigns waged in subsequent decades in such places as Sri Lanka and Algeria during the 1990s.

The January 1968 Tet Offensive (the General Offensive and General Uprising) launched by the Viet Cong and the North Vietnamese military provides dramatic examples of terrorist operations. These occurred at the village level and in the cities of Saigon and Hue especially.

According to captured documents, beginning in November 1967 Viet Cong provincial leaders issued a series of directives calling for the formation of "suicide teams" consisting of 10–20 teenagers, girls as well as boys. These units were then subdivided into three-person cells. They were then to kill local individuals who had been blacklisted as

Table 4.2 US mission reports of Viet Cong assassinations and abductions, 1966–1969

	Assassinations	Abductions
Government officials	1,154	664
Government employees	1,863	381
General populace	15,031	24,862
Subtotal	18,048	25,907
Total 43,955		

Source: Stephen Hosmer, *Viet Cong Repression and Its Implications for the Future* (Lexington, MA: Heath Lexington Books, 1970), p. 44.

government sympathizers. The plan, according to a captured Viet Cong document produced by its head in Ban Me Thuot Province, was as follows:

> Each hamlet where our agents are available should choose from 2 to 3 persons to activate a hamlet uprising section and 2 to 3 suicide cells (selected from among male and female youths) to keep track of and destroy wicked tyrants in the hamlet . . . At present, the conditions are ripe for the implementation of the plan of the Revolution; however the people are controlled by wicked tyrants and administrative personnel in hamlets and villages. If we are able to guide suicide units to kill these wicked tyrants, the people in these villages and hamlets, even though there are no agents present, will rise up to overthrow the enemy government and support and join the Revolution.[35]

Using grenades and daggers, these suicide cells performed two of the classic functions of terrorism. Not only did they eliminate "wicked tyrants" along with "spies" and "traitors" (e.g., Special Forces personnel, rural development cadres, enemy commanders, and pacification personnel) but they also made "propaganda by deed." The killings served as exemplary deeds, especially the self-sacrifice involved, which Viet Cong leaders believed would convert masses of peasants to the cause of revolution. The evidence is fragmentary but these attacks continued through August 1968, after the conclusion of the Tet Offensive.

Viet Cong (and North Vietnamese) terrorism was not confined to rural areas. When the Tet Offensive began at the end of January 1968—the lunar New Year—their forces attacked many cities, including Hue and Saigon. In the case of Hue, the country's historical capital, some 12,000 VC and North Vietnamese forces, labeled the National Liberation Front (NLF), invaded the city and held it or most of it for the next twenty-six days. During this three-week period the NLF set up a new administration charged with purging the city of its old "wicked tyrants" and "reactionary elements." In practice this meant the summary execution of individuals whose names had appeared on lists compiled by VC special activities cells already present in Hue before the attack began.[36]

Douglas Pike, an American foreign service officer stationed in Saigon, reported that the new communist administrators in Hue were accompanied by execution squads. Using clipboards with the names of the blacklisted on them, they quickly rounded up the "wicked tyrants" and reactionaries. The latter were then subject to summary "trials." All the proceedings produced guilty verdicts at ten-minute intervals. Those found guilty were then immediately executed. The killings included religious figures along with Americans and other foreigners. These executions were not the end of things, however. Fearing the worst, large numbers of Hue residents took refuge in a church. A communist official assured them they would be treated fairly and permitted to undergo a re-education program. This assurance turned out not to be true; once outside the church the Vietnamese were killed in a series of massacres.

The VC and North Vietnamese forces were forced out of Hue by a combination of American Marines and South Vietnamese units after a period of fierce fighting that lasted for several weeks. According to Philip Menhard, a US advisor, during their withdrawal from Hue the Viet Cong and North Vietnamese executed all those civilians under their control who refused to depart with them. They regarded Catholics as particular enemies and, consequently, favorite targets. Journalists and other observers differ about the overall number of people killed in this manner. Some Hue residents were no doubt killed in the crossfire between the Americans and ARVN (Armed Forces of the Republic of Vietnam) and the communists seeking to hold the city. Taking account of this fact, it nevertheless seems to be true that close to 2,000 civilians were killed during the attack on Hue as a result of executions.

The VC made no effort to capture Saigon at this time. They did, however, make dramatic efforts to stage terrorist attacks on high prestige or high visibility targets within the city. The VC C-10 Battalion consisting of approximately 250 men and women were sent on suicide missions. (In order to familiarize themselves with Saigon many of them had been working undercover as taxi drivers for some months prior to the attacks.) In what clearly amounted to suicide missions VC teams simultaneously attacked the American Embassy compound (in an unsuccessful attempt to assassinate US Ambassador Ellsworth Bunker), the Vietnamese Joint General Staff headquarters, Navy headquarters, the Presidential Palace (in an attempt to kill South Vietnam's then President Nguyen Van Thieu), the National Broadcasting Station, and Tan Son Nhut Air Base.[37] The American journalist Don Oberdorfer offers this account:

> The Presidential Palace, which is probably the most heavily defended installation in the downtown (Saigon) area, was attacked by a team of thirteen men and a woman . . . In view of the odds against them this was clearly a low-cost attempt at political impact. The sapper team, which arrived in three vehicles, including a truck loaded with TNT, was repelled at the side gate of the palace within a few minutes. The Viet Cong took refuge in an unfinished apartment

building across the street and held out for fifteen hours in a running gun battle until nearly all [sic] of the small unit was killed.[38]

These missions all failed in the sense that the VC was not able to capture and hold these enemy installations for long. On the other hand, they represented classic "propaganda by deed." They conveyed the vulnerability of even highly protected American and South Vietnamese facilities in the country's capital city. Newspaper and television accounts of these attacks were shown all over the United States and helped persuade the American public that there was "no light at the end of the tunnel." There was a difference between perception and reality. By many accounts, the reality was that the VC suffered a major defeat in the Tet Offensive. Many of its units were completely destroyed. (For the remainder of the war it was the North Vietnamese army that had to do the fighting for the communist side.) But in this case the perception was far more important than the reality.

Conclusions

Used as a stand-alone tactic terrorism rarely succeeds in bringing about a strategic victory for its perpetrators. As the experiences of Latin America's "urban guerrillas" and the various revolutionary or pseudo-revolutionary bands active in Europe during the 1970s suggest, endlessly setting off bombs and killing innocent civilians is a hopeless endeavor typically producing public outrage and government repression; sound and fury signifying not much.

On the other hand, terrorist violence may help an insurgent movement achieve success when it is used as simply one of the tactics in its repertoire of coercive measures. Connable and Libicki's data on the outcomes of insurgencies (see p. 90) and our Vietnam War case study confirm this judgment.

How did the terrorist groups end their careers in the tactical and strategic situations described earlier? It really depends on what we mean by "terrorist group." If by the latter we mean the specialized units of larger insurgent organizations they end their careers when they complete the objectives that leaders of the insurgency set for them. Of course there is no causal necessity that insurgent organizations that use terrorism succeed in displacing an incumbent regime. In the aftermath of World War II, communist insurgencies in Malaya and Greece made considerable use of terrorism in their unsuccessful efforts to expel the British from the former and topple the government in Athens in the latter.[39] Those units that perpetrated the terrorist violence shared the fate of their fellow revolutionaries.

In the next chapter we consider the transformation of terrorist organizations. In some cases, the organizations persist, but undergo a metamorphosis into something else. In Chapter 5 we seek to describe what that something else is.

5 Transformation

Many years ago polio was a disease that struck thousands of Americans, particularly young people, every summer. President Franklin Roosevelt was the disease's most famous victim. The March of Dimes was an organization he helped create to raise money in order to fight the disease. During the 1950s researchers developed a vaccine to inoculate people against polio. The vaccination program was a success; after some years, polio virtually disappeared in the United States. The need for the March of Dimes charity seemed to disappear also since its purpose no longer existed. Nevertheless, the organization continues; it now raises money to fight birth defects. The charity persists though its goal has changed.

The same logic may apply in the case of terrorist organizations. Like the March of Dimes, they may undergo a transformation. Terrorism is after all a tactic that groups may adopt but also abandon. They may also continue to employ terrorist violence but in order to achieve some other purpose(s) than the original one.

During the early 1980s, for example, such groups as the Communist Combatant Cells in Belgium and Action Directe in France switched their revolutionary aims from ending capitalist exploitation to preventing NATO from deploying Pershing II and Cruise missiles on European soil. Terrorism was used in effect in support of the peace movement. In other words, the violence persisted but its purpose appeared to change. The terrorist bands were seeking to gain some support among peace groups hoping to create a nuclear-free zone in Western Europe.

Terrorist organizations may also undergo a metamorphosis. Like caterpillars transforming themselves into butterflies or the human being in the short story "Metamorphosis" by Franz Kafka, terrorist groups may abandon the bomb and the gun in favor of other types of political activity. For instance, in Uruguay during the 1960s the Tupamaros waged an urban guerrilla campaign against the government in Montevideo. In 1972 the military intervened and the country was ruled by a junta for the following decade. When democracy was restored, the Tupamaros reappeared, this time as a peaceful political party competing at elections led, for the most part, by the same individuals who led it during its terrorist phase. Much the same may be said in connection with the IRA and Sinn Fein in Northern Ireland (see earlier).

Our purpose in this chapter is to investigate how terrorism or how terrorist groups end by transforming themselves into something else. The else may involve (see above) either a change in aims, a metamorphosis into another type of group, or some combination of both.

Organized crime

Terrorist violence is almost universally regarded by its very nature as a criminal undertaking. In all countries ruled by law murder, kidnap, extortion, and robbery are treated as serious crimes. If they are committed to achieve some political purpose or public good and intended to create terror we typically label these acts as terrorism. If they are perpetrated by an organization to simply achieve a profit, to make money, or some private good, we usually think of these activities as strictly criminal operations. The problem with this distinction is that it often blurs around the edges.[1]

Mexico, for example, is presently caught up in a "drug war" in which various crime organizations, e.g., the Zetas and La Familia, fight for supremacy in the lucrative drug trade with the United States. Although many Mexican citizens living in cities along the country's border with the US are terrified by all the murders going on, sometimes literally, under their windows, we usually don't think of these killings as terrorism. On the other hand, the drug gangs do have a political agenda. The latter involves killing and bribing local political leaders and police officers into permitting the major crime organizations to go about their business undisturbed. If the leaders and police are scared into preferring "silver" over "lead" these organizations will have achieved their political goals.

In thinking about the relationship between crime and politics, we should also consider the question of where terrorists come from. The answer in many cases is prison. In Italy during the 1970s a revolutionary terrorist band, the NAP, was formed from petty criminals in a Neapolitan jail. They had been radicalized by the relevant writings of Frantz Fanon (*The Wretched of the Earth*) and George Jackson (*Soledad Brother*) provided by young, highly educated, middle-class revolutionaries. The same pattern applies to the origins of the Symbionese Liberation Army in the United States, which was formed from a mix of prison inmates and middle-class revolutionaries. Various neo-Nazis in the United States began their careers as "Aryan Warriors" in the penitentiary. And the late Abu Musab al-Zarqawi, leader of al-Qaeda in Iraq, was a petty criminal in Jordan who acquired his religious and political ideals while serving a prison sentence.[2]

Walter Laqueur calls attention to the fact that during periods of unrest criminal elements often join terrorist groups for purposes of looting. He also notes that seizing hostages for money has been a practice from time immemorial. Often the difference between politics and straightforward criminality gets lost in the proceedings.

The IMRO was a terrorist band active in the first decades of the twentieth century committed to the establishment of an independent Macedonia free from Ottoman control. Following the post-World War I peace treaty no such independent state was forthcoming. Macedonian territory was divided among Bulgaria, Greece, and Yugoslavia. IMRO did not disappear, however. Instead it became a murder-for-hire organization receiving an annual subsidy from the Bulgarian and Hungarian governments.[3]

In a more recent case involving Northern Ireland members of the Real IRA robbed the Northern Bank in Belfast in December 2004. They got away with more than £25 million, making it one of the worst robberies in the history of the United Kingdom. Both the Irish and British governments agreed with a police report that members of the Real IRA were responsible for the theft. The robbers though were engaging in a case of free enterprise without any obvious political motivation.

Why the link between terrorism and criminality? The economists Paul Collier and Anke Hoeffler offer us an explanation. In their work on the sources of civil wars they make a distinction between "greed" and "grievance."[4] The question they seek to answer is this: What are the most important factors that make for the outbreak of civil wars? Is it a set of popular grievances linked to economic, religious, and political divisions within a society? Or, is the stimulant more a matter of "greed"?

The assumption Collier and Hoeffler make and then test is that grievances based on these social divisions in society are relatively constant; grievances that accrue around these cleavages are common to many societies, some of which give rise to internal wars while in many other instances they do not. The determining factor, they hypothesize, is the availability of resources with which to wage such an armed struggle. "According to popular perceptions grievances are often seen as the main causes of rebellion. However, we suggest that those factors which determine the military and financial viability of a rebellion are more important than objective grounds for grievance."[5] They suspect, for example, that the exploitation of such natural resources as diamonds in Angola, drugs in Colombia, or copper in the Congo make it easier for rebels to mount and then sustain an insurgency: Access to these resources contributes to a widening in the "opportunity structure" of rebel leaders.[6]

Collier and Hoeffler investigate the occurrence of seventy-eight civil wars (conflicts that cost the lives of more than 1,000 people per year) launched between 1960 and 1999. Their findings, though hardly unambiguous, confirm the strength of the "greed" model in explaining these serious conflicts.

James Fearon, a Stanford political scientist, has investigated the possible linkage between the duration of civil wars and the availability of "contraband" to the rebel forces. He observes that the use by insurgents of income derived from such material as cocaine, precious gems, and opium enhances the ability of rebels to sustain their operations over time.[7]

Rebel groups engaged in a civil war against those in power are not or not necessarily terrorists, though terrorism may be involved as part of their operations. Our concern here though is with the matter of greed. If the acquisition of resources, "greed" (*pace* Gordon Gekko), plays a vital role in terrorist activity, at what point does the pursuit of these resources displace the organization's original political objectives? At what point does resource acquisition become an end in itself rather than a means of achieving the end?

It may strain the imagination to believe that modern terrorist groups, their leaders especially, may be greedy in a personal sense. After all, al-Qaeda leaders Osama bin Laden and Dr Ayman Al-Zawahiri both came from prosperous family backgrounds that they abandoned in favor of a life of severe and conspicuous poverty. The nineteenth-century anarchist Pyotr Kropotkin was a Russian prince. The twentieth-century Italian terrorist leader Giangacomo Feltrinelli was a multi-millionaire publisher. And it is hard to imagine individuals carrying out suicide attacks in order to enrich themselves at least financially.

Why then would terrorists and terrorist organizations committed ostensibly to self-sacrificing ideals develop an interest in financial rewards? Compared to the "greed" incentive for those who have launched a civil war, the material needs of terrorists seem very limited. Even the 9/11 attacks were relatively inexpensive.

Observers may be deceived by the self-serving rhetoric of terrorist spokespersons. Consider this observation Jessica Stern made about several leaders of jihad in Pakistan:

> The terrorists discussed in this chapter boast about successful fundraising efforts not only in the Gulf but also in Iran. One of the leaders

reports that he raised more money than he knows how to use, much of it from Islamist non-government organizations .... Several managers concede that they joined the "jihad" for religious reasons, but that, over time, the salaries they earn have become more important in explaining their loyalty as holy warriors. Several talk about their disenchantment with militancy upon realizing that their leaders were less committed to the cause than to their own financial well-being.[8]

This observation need not be limited to contemporary jihadists. Leaders of the German Red Army Faction (RAF) preferred to steal Mercedes-Benz autos to flee the authorities. Some leaders of the PLO, at least during the group's terrorist phase, enjoyed the high life in France, one of whom was assassinated by Israeli agents in his villa on the Riviera. Likewise Ilich Ramirez Sanchez aka "Carlos the Jackal," a Venezuelan radical who became a terrorist for the Popular Front for the Liberation of Palestine (PFLP) during the 1970s, retired to a seaside villa in Libya following his successful kidnapping of oil ministers at their OPEC headquarters in Vienna in 1975. The various oil-producing member states were willing to pay large ransoms for their release. Carlos' confederates reported that he kept a substantial sum of the money involved for his personal use.[9]

Despite the group's reputation for radical Marxism and heroic self-sacrifice on behalf of the Palestinian cause ("Heroes of the Return"), the PFLP's leader Dr George Habash became a highly successful entrepreneur.[10] During the period of the organization's ascendency in southern Lebanon (1971–1982), the PFLP went into a variety of enterprises, exercising a monopoly over the construction business in Sidon, for example. Was all of this revenue then used to fund the PFLP's operations against Israel?

Personal corruption is one thing or probably one thing, organizational transformation something else. Let us turn our attention to three groups that seem to have undergone or are undergoing such a transformation. Let us consider groups that appear to have replaced political concerns with more pecuniary ones.

The Revolutionary Armed Forces of Colombia (FARC)

FARC, one of the longest surviving insurgencies in Latin America, began in 1965 as a breakaway faction of the Colombian Communist party. Over the years it has been rooted in the country's rural areas, particularly the southeastern part of the country. It has enjoyed substantial support among the peasantry and it combines, like other Latin American revolutionary groups, urban terrorism with guerrilla struggles in the countryside. Ideologically, FARC defines itself as a nationalist organization committed to the elimination of US influence in the region, and that of neo-imperialism more generally. FARC opposes the privatization of Colombia's natural resources. Membership has fluctuated but its estimated numbers range in the thousands.[11] FARC insurgents have also been able to conquer territory in sections of Colombia that have been difficult for the country's armed forces to reach. Sometimes the government in Bogota consented to these land seizures, which, on occasion, amounted to territory the size of Switzerland.

Over the years Colombian governments, since the 1970s, have tried a combination of carrots and sticks, in dealing with FARC and other violent organizations challenging Bogota's authority. Carrots have worked with some of the groups, e.g., amnesty, an opportunity to reenter the political arena, but these measures, despite prolonged peace negotiations, have not succeeded with FARC or the more Marxist-oriented National Liberation Army (ELN).[12] To make matters still worse Colombia has also been plagued by narcotics traffickers, criminal enterprises that market cocaine and other drugs in North America and Europe. As in Mexico, they intervene violently in the political process when their interests are jeopardized. And at least in the recent past there were also right-wing paramilitary groups, hired by wealthy landowners, to wage war against the left-wing revolutionary groups. In the case of FARC the carrots have not worked and recent Colombian governments have adopted a "stick" approach, with some success.

FARC has combined guerrilla warfare tactics with terrorism, both urban and rural. The organization has been responsible for most of the demand for ransom kidnappings in Colombia. The following are suggestive of FARC operations:

The November 2005 kidnapping of sixty people, many of whom are being held hostage by FARC until the government decides to release hundreds of their comrades serving prison sentences.

The February 2002 hijacking of a commercial flight and the kidnapping of a Colombian senator on board.

The February 2002 kidnapping of a Colombian presidential candidate, Ingrid Betancourt, who was traveling in guerrilla territory.

The October 2001 kidnapping and assassination of a former Colombian minister of culture.

The March 1999 murder of three US missionaries working in Colombia.[13]

FARC has derived a significant part of its annual income from the ransom paid for those prominent individuals it kidnapped and then held hostage in its semi-autonomous territory. Bank robberies also make a significant contribution. But the amounts involved pale in comparison to the money FARC has gained through the drug business. One estimate puts the total income derived from narcotics at $100 million per year.

Initially the FARC leadership regarded the drug business as "counter-revolutionary," but as its guerrillas moved into regions of Colombia where coca and poppy farming were prevalent (areas east of the Andes) the attitude changed. This change in outlook was formally ratified at a meeting of the group's Seventh Congress in 1981. The FARC "connection" has taken three forms. First, FARC imposes a tax on small coca farmers in their areas of control. Second, the organization offers protection to lower-rung manufacturers who cook the coca into usable cocaine. And third, FARC helps smuggle the drugs from those parts of Colombia under its control into adjacent countries (though not the major distribution channels to Europe and North America).[14]

In recent years FARC has fallen on hard times. Long-time leaders have died from natural causes or been killed by unnatural ones. Membership has shrunk to a few thousand fighters. Support in the Colombian population is minimal. The chance of FARC achieving its ostensible aim of transforming Colombia via revolution seems increasingly unlikely. FARC has not formally renounced its commitment to revolution. If it did, what purpose could its leaders claim to serve?

Abu Sayyaf

The Abu Sayyaf Group (ASG) is one of a number of groups seeking independence for the heavily Muslim population of the southern Philippines, the island of Mindanao especially, from the Christian-dominated government in Manila. ASG's leaders hoped to go beyond an independent Islamic state and participate in the formation of a regional caliphate including Indonesia, Singapore, Malaysia, and other parts of Southeast Asia.[15]

ASG dates its formation to 1991 when its founder, Abdurajik Abubakar Janjalini, a Philippine academic (later killed in a shootout with the police) who studied in Libya and Egypt, rejected the compromises involving regional autonomy reached by the Moro National Liberation Front (MNLF) and the Moro Islamic Liberation Front (MILF) with the Manila government. ASG's first fighters were drawn from MILF. Later some of the ASG jihadists received training at al-Qaeda camps in Afghanistan.

Unlike FARC, ASG had few natural resources on which to draw. Over time its income has come from bank robberies and kidnapping for ransom operations. And if the ransom was not paid, ASG has from time to time beheaded those victims in its control. The organization's effective leader during the 1990s and early years of the current century was Aldam Tilao. The American journalist Mark Bowden describes Tilao as follows:

> [a] stocky and gregarious figure with a round face, smooth brown skin, and a receding hairline that he disguised somewhat by shaving his head and topping it with a beret or wrapping it in a black do-rag like an American hip-hop artist. With his single hoop earring and Oakley sunglasses, he affected the look of a Hollywood pirate . . . Tilao was a criminal, and to him Islam was just the latest cover for a lifetime of increasingly violent thuggery . . . Taking the name Abu Sabaya ("Bearer of Captives"), he began a campaign of kidnapping, rape and murder, and emerged as the spokesman for and most visible face of the Abu Sayyaf movement. Tilao became a frequent voice on the radio in Mindanao, and he apparently so enjoyed this public persona that he nicknamed himself "DJ," embroidering the initials on his backpack.[16]

Tilao's love of attention proved his undoing. His visibility made it easier for the Philippine military to track him down and kill him in the inevitable gun battle. ASG survives, however. His successors have sought—how successfully remains to be seen—to restore the organization's commitment to mass murder on behalf of religious ideals.

These episodes include the 2004 firebombing of a Philippine ferry (Superferry14) that killed 116 passengers and a series of motorcycle assassinations in August 2006 that left seventy people dead. ASG also planned attacks on the 2007 summit meetings of the Association of Southeast Asian Nations (ASEAN) and the organization of East Asian nations. However, ASG was not able to bring these schemes to fruition.[17]

Despite the effort to burnish the ASG's religious credentials, former captives recall these

> jihadists to be shallow, even adolescent, in their faith. Unfamiliar with the Koran, the outlaws had only a sketchy notion of Islam, which they saw as a set of behavioral rules, to be violated when it suited them. Kidnapping, murder, and theft were justified by their special status as "holy warriors."[18]

Abu Nidal and the Fatah Revolutionary Council

Sabri Khalil al-Banna or Abu Nidal was a Palestinian militant (born in 1937 in Jaffa during the period of the British Mandate) who went through a period of radicalization during his formative years in refugee camps in the Gaza Strip and Nablus, in the then Jordanian West Bank. Later he moved to Saudi Arabia where he found work with a construction company. In the early 1960s Abu Nidal joined the Ba'ath party, the pan-Arab organization that was later to seize power in Iraq and Syria. Sometime later he organized a group of young Palestinians to wage war, at least rhetorically, against the Israeli enemy. For this effort he was fired from his job with ARAMCO, the oil company. He then returned to Nablus where he joined Yassir Arafat's Fatah organization.[19]

Until the June 1967 war and Israel's conquest of the West Bank, Abu Nidal's involvement in Fatah had been limited. The effect of Israel's occupation of Nablus apparently had a transformative effect, turning Abu Nidal into a terrorist with an unwavering hatred of the Jewish state. Armed with this hatred Abu Nidal and his band of followers organized a series of attacks on Israeli targets marked, as his biographer Patrick Seale notes, by their random cruelty.[20]

Until 1974 the Abu Nidal organization remained under the PLO umbrella as part of Fatah. But following the PLO's decision that year to pursue a path of negotiations with Israel, he led his followers out from under the umbrella to pursue a policy relying exclusively on terrorist violence. This position won Abu Nidal the support of Ba'athist-controlled Iraq. The latter had even refused a UN sponsored ceasefire between Israel and the Arab states. At this point Iraq offered sanctuary and sponsorship to Abu Nidal's Fatah Revolutionary Council.[21]

It is true that following his decision to pursue a separate course his followers carried out a series of attacks on Israeli and Jewish targets. These attacks included the machine-gunning of worshippers at a synagogue in Istanbul (1986) and the El Al ticket counters at the Rome and Vienna airports (1986). Despite Abu Nidal's hatred of Israel, from his break with Fatah onwards, most of his group's terrorism was directed against Arab targets. A summary would include the following:

October 1974—Abu Nidal agents try to kill Fatah leader Mahmud Abbas (Abu Massin).

January 1978—Sa'id Hammami, PLO representative in London and a well-known dove, is killed by an Abu Nidal gunman.

June 1978—Ali Yassin, PLO representative in Kuwait, is killed by an Abu Nidal gunman.

August 1978—Izz al-Din Qalaq, PLO representative in Paris, is killed by an Abu Nidal gunman.

July 1981—Abu Dawud, the Fatah guerrilla commander, narrowly survives an attack on his life in Warsaw by an Abu Nidal gunman.[22]

Abu Iyad, a co-founder of Fatah, was not so lucky, however. In 1991 he was assassinated by an Abu Nidal agent in Tunis. The agent had been working as a PLO security guard at the organization's headquarters.

Why all the killing of other Palestinians by Abu Nidal? Was it sheer hatred of the PLO's decision to consider negotiations with Israel that propelled Abu Nidal's group to embark on this fratricidal course?

The answer is no. No one can deny that this "master terrorist" hated Yassir Arafat (he was hardly alone in this regard). What happened was that Abu Nidal became a "hired gun" for three Arab governments: Iraqi, Syrian, and Libyan. Each of the regimes in Baghdad, Damascus, and Tripoli offered Abu Nidal sanctuary, weapons, and cash in exchange for his group's willingness to carry out their instructions.

In effect Abu Nidal's group became an instrument in the foreign policies of these radical regimes. It would target figures in Fatah and other PLO groups and certain Arab governments (e.g., Saudi Arabia) based on the prevailing objectives of Saddam Hussein, Colonel Qaddafi, and Hafez al-Asad. Eventually Abu Nidal was the victim of one of his patrons. Saddam Hussein had him killed in the lead-up to the March 2003 US invasion of Iraq. Abu Nidal and his organization had outlived its usefulness.

We should not conclude this part of our discussion without paying some attention to the struggle presently under way in Afghanistan and Pakistan. Afghanistan is, after all, the largest poppy-growing region in the world. And both countries have long histories of drug smuggling and other forms of organized crime. It would be surprising if the forces challenging the governments in Kabul and Islamabad were indifferent to the drug business. And indeed they are not.

In both countries the term "Taliban" refers to multiple groups, few of which enjoy harmonious relations with their counterparts. The Quetta Shura and the Haqqani (headquartered in Pakistan's Federally Administered Tribal Areas) network along with al-Qaeda are the key actors in the Afghan insurgency. In Pakistan al-Qaeda has developed ties to three indigenous terrorist bands, Lashkar-e-Taiba, Jaish-e-Mohammed, and Lashkar-e-Islami (largely a drug gang using Islamism as a cover), groups that in the past at least received support from the military's inter-services intelligence agency (ISI). The Pakistani Taliban is divisible into the main organization located in the Federally Administered Tribal Areas and the Punjab Taliban who reflect the non-Pashtun elements in the overall organization. If we add to this mix various tribal groups, straightforward criminal organizations, and internal rivalries within the Taliban structures we confront a relatively complicated insurgent environment.

Unlike FARC, which has derived a substantial income from taxing or extorting money from coca farmers, the Afghan and Pakistani groups have gone into other elements of the drug business as well. They now engage in processing and refining poppies into heroin and opium and then smuggling the drugs to distribution sites in Pakistan and adjacent countries. Vast amounts of money are involved.[23]

Spokesmen for the various Taliban organizations say the drug money is needed to help the "holy warriors" achieve their lofty religious goals aimed at establishing or reestablishing an emirate in the region. But observers, both Afghan and Pakistani, express skepticism:

> Following the arrest of a number of leading Afghan drug traffickers, senior Taliban commanders in the south appear to be taking a broader role in the drug trade, moving into the more profitable processing and exporting end of the business, and shifting their focus off of taxing poppy farmers and drug convoys. This shift in focus from farm level taxation to the processing and exporting end of the drug trade indicates the QST (Quetta Shura Taliban) is behaving more like a drug cartel. US law enforcement and military officials are now [2010] tracking more than three dozen separate smuggling operations, many of which appear to answer directly to the QST.[24]

The pursuit of drug profits has contributed to the insurgents' growing unpopularity. Many Afghans have come to dislike the Taliban groups because of their evident hypocrisy—the difference between rhetoric and reality—something Jessica Stern noticed in her interviews with various leaders (see p. 99). Many Afghans also oppose the Karzai government in Kabul not only because it is itself corrupt but also because of its inability to protect their communities against the depredations of the Taliban.

None of the terrorist groups to which we have referred would depict themselves other than in terms that would make Robin Hood and His Merry Men blush. Reality though seems to reveal a different, more complex story. This story reflects a mix of motives both among the various groups and among their members. For some the ideology or theology serves as a rationalization for more material interests, while for "true believers" the sentiments they express, e.g., hatred and the desire for revenge, seem more genuine. Whatever the mix, the organizations we have sought to describe continue to carry out terrorist attacks but the purposes behind them appear to be undergoing a transformation from the pursuit of political or religious ideas to more pecuniary objectives. Instead of collaborating with organized criminal groups, as time passes they seem to transform themselves: more crime, less politics.

Party politics

Is it true that "once a terrorist always a terrorist"? The answer is no, as the world abounds with individuals who have retired from terrorism to pursue other careers and live perfectly normal lives. For many being a terrorist was a brief experience, a phase. For instance, Dipak Gupta, who now teaches peace studies at San Diego State University, was a member of the Naxalites, the Indian terrorist group, in his youth. Antonio Negri resumed his career as a political philosopher after having been jailed by the Italian authorities for his role in Autonomia, a group committed to armed spontaneity. Some terrorists undergo a metamorphosis and reappear later as nonviolent political leaders. Dilma Rousseff, the first woman president of Brazil, spent her early years as a terrorist active in the clandestine Revolutionary Armed Vanguard when her country was ruled by the military. Both former Israeli prime ministers Menachem Begin and Yitzak Shamir were leaders of terrorist groups, the Irgun and the Fighters for the Freedom of Israel (Lehi), in their youth. The former even shared the Nobel Peace Prize with Yassir Arafat, leader of the Palestinian Fatah organization during its terrorist phase. Other individuals might be mentioned.

If this observation applies to individuals it also applies in the case of terrorist groups. Some have undergone transformations from bombs and bullets to the ballot box. The most obvious example (see pp. 25–28) is that of the IRA's abandonment of violence in favor of party political competition as the Sinn Fein following the 1998 Good Friday agreement.[25]

The opposite relationship though from ballot box to bombs and bullets is more common. Political parties or, more frequently, factions within political parties become terrorist groups. Sometimes the relationship between party politics and terrorism is simultaneous with a political party giving rise to a clandestine terrorist apparatus and a terrorist group developing an open political wing to better communicate its views to the public. On other occasions the linkage between party politics and terrorism changes over time. The relationship between terrorism and electoral competition may change with shifting circumstances. The history of Irish republicanism may serve as an illustration. The two tactics, terrorist violence and electoral competition, may shift back and forth depending on how leaders perceive the advantages of one or the other. In this section of the chapter our focus is on shifts from terrorism to party politics with some comments about situations where groups engage in both tactics simultaneously.[26] We should also note that the switch from terrorism to party politics need not be permanent. On occasion groups may revert to the "armed struggle" when they have not obtained what they expected from the political arena.

We also need to remind ourselves that terrorist groups, like political parties, are often divided into factions. Leaders of some faction(s) may advocate a return to party politics while the heads of others retain a commitment to the "armed struggle." The history of the Basque group ETA illustrates this pattern. Over its long experience using terrorist violence, one faction after another has peeled off to pursue the goal of Basque independence from Spain through the ballot box and parliamentary lobbying.[27]

Irgun

The protracted struggle between Israelis and Palestinians provides us with a rich series of examples of a shift from terrorism to conventional party politics. During the British Mandate over Palestine in the years leading up to and following World War II two Jewish terrorist groups emerged: the Irgun and the Lehi (or Stern Gang).[28] Their principal aim was to force the British to leave Palestine so that an independent Jewish state could be established, one free of Arab dominance as well. Irgun had been formed to defend members of the Mandate's Jewish community following the Arab rioting of 1929 that had led to the deaths of some hundreds of Jews. The organization was an offshoot of the Revisionist Zionist movement, followers of the dissident nationalist Ze'ev Jabotinsky. The Lehi in turn was formed by Irgun dissidents headed by Avraham Stern, following the latter's decision in 1940 to avoid attacking British targets during Britain's life-and-death struggle with Nazi Germany.[29]

The catalyst for this break was the British government's decision to issue a White Paper in August 1939 severely restricting Jewish immigration to Palestine. The context for this government policy was the brewing war in Europe and the increasing ferocity of the Nazis' persecution of the European Jewish community. Once World War II broke out in September, Irgun suspended its "military" campaign to compel the

British to abandon the Mandate—reasoning that nothing should be done to weaken the war effort against Hitler. Stern (later killed in a gun battle with the British) and his followers, a minority of a minority in other words, thought otherwise.

During the war, particularly after the Anglo-American victory in North Africa in 1943, Lehi carried out a series of attacks on British targets: these included a failed assassination attempt on Sir Harold MacMichael, the Commissioner for Palestine, and a successful one in Cairo against Lord Moyne, his country's Higher Commissioner for the Middle East. Irgun, on the other hand, held its fire until the war ended in 1945 and the announcement by Britain's new Labour government to continue the White Paper's exclusionary policy. It was at this point that Begin and Irgun launched their revolt against a continuation of British rule.

Until the United Nations' November 1947 decision to partition Palestine, Irgun waged a terrorist campaign aimed at making the cost of Britain's continued presence outweigh whatever benefit (i.e., protecting the Suez Canal) accrued to its retention of control. The most spectacular of Irgun's attacks was the bombing of the King David Hotel in Jerusalem in 1946. One wing of the hotel, housing Britain's administrative head-quarters, was demolished, leaving ninety-one people dead.[30] The attack was condemned by leaders of the Jewish community in Palestine as an act of barbarism. Leaders of the Hagganah, the community's official militia, participated in the effort to track down those responsible for the bombing.

The months between November 1947 and Israel's declaration of independence in April 1948 witnessed an armed struggle between the Jewish and Arab militia groups for supremacy as the Mandate came to an end and as the British prepared to withdraw. In this context, both sides to the fighting carried out terrorist attacks on each other's civilian populations, with Irgun playing a leading role in this regard.

Following April 1948 the newly declared state of Israel was attacked by the armed forces of the surrounding Arab countries. During this first Arab–Israeli war, both Irgun and Lehi participated in the fighting but played small roles compared to the newly formed conventional armed forces. In the war, Lehi assassinated the Swedish diplomat Folke Bernadotte, there on a UN peacekeeping mission. Also during the war, Irgun fighters carried out the well-known massacre of Arab civilians in the town of Deir Yassin, a community on the road between Tel Aviv and Jerusalem.

Following the 1949 truce agreement, both Lehi and Irgun transformed themselves into parliamentary political parties. Ex-members of Lehi formed the Fighters' Party, which survived until 1951, having managed to win one seat in the Israeli parliament. The Herut (Freedom) Party was much more successful. Set up by Begin to represent the ultra-nationalist views of revisionist Zionism, it repudiated all negotiations with the Arab states. Begin and his followers believed in an Israel that would stretch from the Mediterranean to the Jordan, including all the biblical "land of Israel." It was also a party that advocated free enterprise and capitalism as against the then ruling Labor Party's commitment to democratic socialism.

For at least the first decade of its participation in democratic elections and parliamentary deliberations Herut was ostracized by the other parties. Begin, in particular, was despised by the country's first prime minister David Ben-Gurion. Despite or perhaps because of this ostracism, the Herut managed to endure and as the years passed its voter support increased; from a right-wing fringe party it became a major player in Israeli politics. From the late 1950s on it became the second-strongest party in the Knesset, Israel's parliament. Later it merged with the Liberal Party and, in 1967, as the country prepared for its next war with the Arab states, Begin was brought into an all-party coalition government. In the years following the Six Day War, Herut merged with more parties to form the Likud. This Likud alliance won the 1977 national elections. Menachem Begin became Israel's prime minister. Later still he entered into the Camp David peace accords with Egypt's President Sadat, with both winning the Nobel Peace Prize as the result.[31]

Fatah

The conflict between Israel and the Arab states surrounding it had largely been dormant in the decade after the October 1956 Sinai war between the former and Egypt. We might say something similar in regard to the cause of Palestinian nationalism. Followers of Haj Amin al-Husseini, the Grand Mufti of Jerusalem, had succeeded in assassinating Abdullah, King of Jordan, in 1951 out of fear he would negotiate a peace agreement with the Israelis. In the aftermath of this killing there is not much to report. At the end of the 1950s there were stirrings. Student politics was the source of this awakening or reawakening. In Beirut Dr George Habash, a physician trained at the American University, created the Arab National Movement (ANM), a group committed to the cause of Pan-Arabism, for whom the elimination of Israel was part of a larger cause. Under Habash's leadership the ANM gave rise to the PFLP, a Marxist group that was to play a major role in the terrorist violence of the 1970s.

Fatah ("Victory" or "Conquest") was also the product of student politics during the 1950s. At the University of Cairo Yassir Arafat, a young engineering student, became the leader of a Palestinian student organization. After earning his degree, Arafat moved to Kuwait where he went into business with several other young Palestinians. In 1959 they organized Fatah as a nationalist group whose primary interest was the destruction of Israel and its replacement by a Palestinian state.[32] To a considerable extent Arafat and other members of this "vanguard" organization saw violence as the almost exclusive device to be used in mobilizing the Palestinian masses, particularly those living in refugee camps in Lebanon, Syria, and Jordan. The author of an early Fatah statement was nothing if not explicit: "Blazing our armed revolution inside the occupied territory [i.e., Israel] is a healing medicine for all our people's diseases."[33]

The model on which the armed revolution was to be based was the Algerian war (1954–1962) and the inspirational writings of Franz Fanon with his views on the therapeutic benefits of violence against colonists occupying the homeland. Inspirational or not, Fatah began to launch attacks inside Israel in the mid-1960s. Arafat and his fedayeen's immediate hope were to provoke a war between Israel and the Arab states. In other words Fatah's strategy was to attack targets inside Israel. The Israelis would then retaliate against Jordan and Syria and consequently create a spiral of conflict leading to an all-out war.

The outcome of the war was obvious. Israel would be destroyed and the Israelis pushed into the sea. Fatah succeeded in helping at least to provoke just such a war. But its outcome was not what the Fatah leaders had hoped.

The aptly named Six Day War of June 1967 had far-ranging consequences so far as the Palestinian cause was concerned. Israel's rapid victory over its Arab enemies led Palestinian leaders to rethink their position. The idea that conventional means of armed force would lead to the Jewish state's downfall had proved erroneous. The leaders concluded they would have to depend on their own means to achieve victory.

What followed was the reconstruction of the PLO.[34] Originally the PLO had been an organization created by the Egyptian leader Gamel Nasser in 1964 to counter Syrian support for Fatah. In 1968 the Palestinian leadership transformed it into an umbrella organization under which all or most of the emerging violent national liberation groups would find a haven. Yassir Arafat as the head of the largest of these groups became the chairman of the PLO. Article 9 of the PLO's 1968 Covenant reads:

Armed struggle is the only way to liberate Palestine and is therefore
a strategy and not tactics. The Palestinian Arab people affirm its
absolute resolution and abiding determination to pursue the armed
struggle and to march forward towards the armed popular revolution,
to liberate its homeland.[35]

In other words, the PLO had no interest in discussions, negotiations, and
compromises with the Zionist enemy. Conventional party politics was
the furthest thing from its leaders' minds. But what then did "armed
struggle" mean?

In the case of the PFLP it meant launching terrorist attacks in West
European countries and in the skies above them, as airline skyjackings
became its emblematic form of operation. For Fatah, on the other hand,
it meant forays into the Israeli-controlled West Bank and into Israel
proper. These attacks though did not, at least initially, have the desired
inspirational effect on the Palestinian masses. What seemed to have such
an effect was Israel's March 1968 retaliatory raid on Karameh, Fatah's
regional headquarters inside Jordan. Israeli forces suffered casualties and
were compelled to sustain the fighting for some hours. Karameh was
defined as a PLO victory by the organization's spokesmen. The ensuing
publicity created enthusiasm among many Palestinians for the struggle
and produced thousands of recruits to participate in it.

The PLO groups in Jordan under Arafat's leadership soon began to
act as a state within a state, much to the displeasure of King Hussein and
his largely Bedouin army. War erupted in September 1970 ("Black
September") and ended almost a year later with the PLO's defeat and
departure for Lebanon, an even more fragile political entity. From 1971
until its expulsion from the country in 1982, the various PLO factions
were headquartered in Beirut. They also came to control much of
southern Lebanon—which came to be known as "Fatahland."

It was during this decade that Fatah and other PLO groups achieved
widespread recognition for their numerous terrorist operations. These
included attacks both inside Israel and in Europe. The most spectacular
of these events was the attack of "Black September" on Israeli athletes
at their dormitory during the 1972 Munich Olympics. Black September
was a *nom de guerre* Arafat had given to this terrorist band in order to
preserve Fatah's ability to deny it was staging attacks on civilian targets,
far from Israel proper.

The results of the 1973 war between Egypt, Syria, and Israel led
to a series of disengagement agreements leading eventually to a full-
fledged peace treaty between two of the three warring parties. These
developments did not leave Fatah and the PLO unaffected. In 1974 the

PLO National Council expressed a willingness to enter discussions with the aim of establishing a Palestinian state on the West Bank and Gaza Strip. This new state would be the first stage in a process leading to the replacement of Israel by a unified Palestine from the Mediterranean to the Jordan. But this "concession" aroused the opposition of the so-called rejectionist front consisting of the PFLP and other Marxist groups heretofore under the PLO umbrella. Syria backed the dissidents by opposing all reference to talk and negotiations.

If we drew a balance sheet for Fatah and the PLO more generally at this point it would look like this. On the plus side, the organizations had won recognition at the United Nations as a legitimate national entity. The PLO had achieved diplomatic recognition by many states, particularly in the Third World and the Communist bloc. The situation of the Palestinians had caught the world's attention. On the negative side of the balance sheet, the various PLO factions had become embroiled in the Lebanese Civil War from 1975 forward. Despite spectacular acts of terrorism inside Israel and in Europe, the "armed struggle" had not brought the PLO or Arafat any closer to achieving their territorial aims.

In fact, the PLO's attacks on Israelis led to its expulsion from Lebanon. In 1982, following its peace agreement with Egypt, Israeli forces invaded Lebanon and compelled the PLO groups, at least their leadership, to leave the country. The PLO reestablished its headquarters in Tunisia, over 1,000 miles from the site of its struggle. At this point the organization was looking increasingly irrelevant, as new religious groups Hamas and PIJ took up the struggle.

This struggle manifested itself in the largely spontaneous outbreak of the first Intifada in December 1987, a popular and violent protest against Israeli control of the occupied territories. Against this background Arafat and the PLO sought to open discussions with the United States. The price the US asked in return was a commitment by the PLO to abandon terrorism and a willingness to settle for a two-state solution to the conflict.

Arafat and his dominant Fatah faction within the PLO expressed a willingness to pay this price. In November 1988 the PLO National Council passed a resolution accepting UN Resolutions 242 and 338, statements that called for a peaceful solution to the conflict and the recognition of all states in the region including Israel. The PLO resolution also called for an international conference to settle matters. On the basis of this and other assurances the US began a dialogue with Arafat.[36]

In the wake of the 1990–1991 war between Saddam Hussein's Iraq and the US-led alliance arrayed against it, the Bush administration sponsored a conference in Madrid to discuss outstanding Middle East issues. The Israeli government, headed by former Lehi leader Yitzhak Shamir, objected to direct PLO participation, so a Palestinian group participated as part of the Jordanian delegation.

The ensuing talks between Israeli and Palestinian representatives, some public, others secret, led to the 1993 Oslo Accords involving mutual recognition, with the PLO recognizing Israel's legitimacy and the latter (the Israeli side was now represented by a Labor-coalition government headed by Yitzhak Rabin) doing likewise with the PLO.

The Oslo Accords led to the formation of the Palestinian Authority (PA) the following year. Arafat was elected the PA's first president. In 1996 the Israelis withdrew from some 30 percent of Palestinian territory, including Jericho, most of the Gaza Strip, and the major towns on the West Bank. These withdrawals made possible elections for a new parliament, the Palestinian Legislative Council (PLC). Fatah reconstituted itself as a political party and won the majority of seats in the new body. Moreover many of its candidates represented a new generation of Palestinians, individuals who had not gone through the "armed struggle" phase of its operations.[37]

At this point it seemed as if the entire conflict might be heading for a final, compromise-based, resolution. Unfortunately this was not to be the case. Fatah and the PA were challenged by two Islamist groups, Hamas and PIJ, who did what they could to sabotage the peace process. Suicide bombings became their specialty. These terrorist attacks served to infuriate the Israelis and, as Hamas and PIJ hoped, undercut support for the peace process. Eventually, there was a reescalation of the struggle during the late 1990s culminating with the outbreak of the Al-Aqsa Intifada in the fall of 2000. Where did these developments leave Fatah?

The answer is that it remained a political party seeking to retain its dominant role in the PA and the PLC but its situation became increasingly precarious. In order to maintain its radical credentials vis-à-vis challenges from Hamas and PIJ, Fatah militants created the al-Aqsa Martyrs' Brigades that launched a series of terrorist attacks on Israeli targets in the years following the outbreak of this second Intifada. On the other hand, and simultaneously, it pursued a role as a political party, offering patronage benefits to a selective Palestinian clientele and occupying positions of power, thanks to Arafat, throughout the PA.

In some ways Fatah in its transformation from a terrorism-based insurgency to a corrupted ruling political party resembled many Third World liberation movements. Success of an "armed struggle" means the departure of an occupying power, institutionalization of the movement as it comes to rule the new country, followed by the loss of militancy and more mundane efforts to retain power and the material benefits that accrue with its possession. (A host of sub-Saharan African states fit this description.)

Fatah's situation was unusual in a number of ways. Its Hamas and PIJ opponents received substantial support from outside powers, Iran most notably, opposed to any solution other than Israel's obliteration. In this regard Fatah's opponents appear to enjoy widespread support from elements in the Palestinian population both in the "territories" and in the Diaspora. This made it too difficult for Fatah to engage in the normal types of police and military repression employed with such success in the Middle East and other places in the Third World. Finally, the Israelis by and large did not see themselves as interlopers from Europe. Rather they believed the "Zionist project" was itself another national liberation movement engaged in a struggle though of a somewhat different kind.

Hezbollah

Hezbollah (or the Party of God, a reference to a verse in the Koran) emerged in the midst of the Lebanese civil war (1975–1989) and in the wake of Israel's invasion of its northern neighbor in 1982. Despite these crucial events, Hezbollah's formation probably would not have occurred without the Iranian Revolution of 1979 and the ascent of the Ayatollah Khomeini's promotion of Shiite militancy in the Middle East and beyond.

Historically, Lebanon's Shiite population had been large but economically deprived and politically under-represented. Prior to the major events just mentioned, the Shia community had undergone a political awakening under the charismatic leadership of Musr al-Sadr, an Iranian educated cleric. Before he was killed (evidently by Libyan agents) in 1978 al-Sadr founded the Movement of the Deprived and the militia Amal to which it was linked. Amal pursued a middle-of-the-road course in seeking the expansion of Shiite influence while seeking good relations with other Lebanese denominations.[38]

The Iranian Revolution and the Israeli invasion provided the catalysts for what followed, as young Shiite radicals coalesced around the cause. In 1982 many of these young militants received training in Lebanon's Bqaa Valley by members of Iran's Revolutionary Guards. But, "although its members refer to 1982 as the year the group was founded, Hezbollah did not exist as a coherent organization until the mid-1980s. From 1982 through the mid-1980s it was less an organization than a cabal."[39]

What existed instead were a number of small groups including Islamic Amal, often using the generic name "Islamic Jihad" for the purposes of carrying out a number of terrorist operations. The most spectacular of these operations were the suicide bombings of the American and French Embassies in Beirut and the US Marine Corp barracks near that city's international airport in 1983.

The context for these attacks was the presence of a MNF consisting of American, French, British, and Italian contingents sent to Lebanon following the massacre of Palestinian civilians in refugee camps by Christian militia men backed by the Israeli military. The latter had forced PLO fighters to leave Beirut thereby leaving the civilians unprotected.

The problem was that the MNF got caught up in the Lebanese civil war (see pp. 81–82). It was identified with the Christian-based Lebanese army and consequently the MNF became seen as an enemy for many Shia living in Beirut's slums.[40] Following the MNF's withdrawal from Lebanon the following year, it became clear that Hezbollah had become a magnet for thousands of young Shiite militants inspired by the Iranians and led by Sheik Mohammed Fadlallah, its spiritual adviser, and a young high school chemistry teacher Abbas al-Musawi who, until he was assassinated by the Israelis, put his knowledge of chemistry to use helping to make bombs.

In fact Hezbollah pioneered the use of suicide bombings as a terrorist tactic. During the period 1983–1985 not only did suicide "martyrs" attack MNF targets but Israeli ones as well.[41] In the Israeli case, as with the MNF, suicide attacks contributed to its decision to retreat to a narrow "security zone" in the southern part of Lebanon.

In addition to martyrdom operations, Hezbollah figures engaged in a number of other terrorist attacks, including the kidnapping and killing of various Western hostages. Perhaps the most widely publicized of these attacks was the 1985 skyjacking of TWA Flight 847 bound from Athens to Rome in which the Shia terrorists killed one and tortured several of its passengers.

As it grew in its level of popular support, Hezbollah evolved from small bands of street fighters and clandestine terrorists into a mass organization, one heavily subsidized by the Iranians. Following the end of the Lebanese civil war in 1988–1989, Hezbollah's leaders, chief of whom were Sheik Fadlallah (recently deceased) and Hasan Nasrallah, decided to participate in electoral politics. From 1992 forward, the "party of God" has become a less divine political party, competing in both local and national elections. Its strength in parliament has increased over the years. Its popular support at the polls became sufficiently strong so that by 2005 it achieved membership in the country's ruling coalition. Some Hezbollah figures now serve as cabinet ministers, with responsibility for administering various government departments.[42]

Hezbollah however has not traded the bomb and gun for the ballot box. What has occurred instead is that it has combined electoral participation with a dramatically enhanced capacity for violence. Hezbollah militia groups, relying largely on guerrilla tactics, inflicted a sufficiently high number of casualties on Israeli soldiers so that Yehud Barak's government was compelled to make the decision in 2000 to completely withdraw from its "security zone" in southern Lebanon. Since that year Hezbollah has acquired a meaningful war-fighting capacity. Equipped with Iran-supplied missiles Hezbollah was able to sustain a military campaign with Israel for over a month in 2006, a fight in which thousands of Israelis were forced to flee from the northern part of the country as Hezbollah fighters launched missiles at Haifa and other significant targets.

The US state department labels Hezbollah a terrorist organization. West European governments have been more reluctant to apply the term. This American versus European difference reflects the ambiguity of the organization itself. It is Janus-faced in the sense that it is committed to Israel's destruction by violent military means and it stages terrorist attacks from time to time inside Lebanon in order to deal with its domestic rivals. On the other hand, it is a political party with a cabinet-level presence and an organizational apparatus that includes its own television station and a set of such social welfare institutions as hospitals, community centers, and schools. Of course there is no requirement that Hasan Nasrallah and the rest of the Hezbollah leadership make it easier on Western governments by deciding to abandon violence in favor of peaceful party political activity or give up the former for the latter. Barring dramatic changes in outlook by its patrons, the regimes in Iran and Syria, Hezbollah seems likely to combine violence and party politics, with a subordinate role for terrorist operations.

Conclusions

Oftentimes groups that employ terrorism as a tactic seek to destabilize governments and other institutions. We should consider the possibility that by the use of terrorist violence they may inadvertently destabilize themselves. There are some exceptions involving groups that persist in staging terrorist attacks over long periods of time without any major impact either on society, the government, or their own membership. For example, the Greek group Revolutionary Organization November 17 persisted in assassinating American, Turkish, NATO, and Greek officials on a relatively regular basis between 1975 and 2000. Most members were arrested in the lead-up to the summer Olympic Games staged in Athens in the latter year. November 17 had hoped to spark a revolution, but the effort failed to ignite one. When its demise occurred, the authorities discovered that the group's membership had been relatively constant over the decades. Youthful revolutionaries had persisted, on a part-time basis, well into middle age.

This chapter, on the other hand, has focused on terrorist groups that have undergone or are in the process of undergoing a transformation. We pointed out that the changes involved may go in one of two directions. It is an oversimplification to be sure, but we think it is common for some groups to persist in their use of violence but to shift their aims from political to pecuniary. Groups and individual members are unlikely to announce publicly that they are now more interested in making money than achieving some religious or political objective.

For the most part terrorist groups are voluntary. Members persist in their efforts because they receive some benefit in exchange. These incentives may be social or psychological, e.g., belonging to a group of like-minded individuals, embarking on an exciting adventure, achieving revenge, carrying out the will of God. Over time however these benefits may lose their ability to inspire violent action: When disillusionment and boredom set in, more material considerations may displace the older incentives, both for individual members and for the group as a whole. Public rhetoric may obscure this reality, at least for a while.

The second circumstance that we have considered in this chapter is one of organizational transformation. The group, or an armed faction within it, abandons the use of terrorism in favor of conventional party politics activity. What had been the political wing of a terrorist group comes to dominate the group as a whole. And its tactical focus shifts to competing at elections and winning votes. What seem most likely to bring about this type of terrorist group to political party transformation are changes in its structure of opportunity. Offers of amnesty by the government, as in Colombia, coupled with an unfettered chance to participate in elections, provide opportunities that theretofore were missing. The same may be said in some instances when countries undergo transitions from colonial or authoritarian rule to democracy. The transformations of the Irgun into the Herut, and Fatah from terrorist organization into ruling political party (see p. 108), offer compelling illustrations.

In sum, terrorist campaigns seem to set in motion inherently unstable conditions. As a result in at least some of the cases involved these conditions lead the groups involved to undergo major transformations either in their aims, their forms of organization, or both.

6 Conclusions

What is the future of terrorism and of those groups that currently wage terrorist campaigns, at least as we have come to understand these concepts? There are certainly nightmare scenarios to contemplate. As we noted earlier, in October 2010, US President Obama mentioned the worst possibility: nuclear terrorism.[1] He is hardly the first American leader or terrorism specialist to issue such a warning.[2] In fact, the worries go back decades, as international terrorism became a serious concern with the advent of airliner skyjackings in the early 1970s.

Usually the fears of terrorist groups acquiring nuclear weapons have been linked to the initials WMD, weapons of mass destruction. These include chemical, biological, and radiological weapons along with the possible use of "the Bomb." Terrorists would detonate or disperse such weapons in hopes of killing as many people as their destructive powers would permit. These fears were heightened by the Japanese cult Aum Shinrikyo's dispersion of sarin gas in the Tokyo subway system in 1995, an attack that killed a dozen passengers. Some terrorism observers in the US concluded that a threshold had been crossed and that subsequently authorities in the democracies would have to defend their populations against WMD.

But this threat has not been transformed into reality, at least not yet. In the years following the Aum Shinrikyo attack, terrorists have certainly managed to kill large numbers of people, but without the benefit of WMD. Instead, for example, box cutters were used by al-Qaeda operatives to seize control of four commercial airliners on 9/11 and then crash three of them into the World Trade Center and the Pentagon. No WMD but the death toll was about 3,000.

Conventional weapons have been used to inflict mass casualties but with a new wrinkle: suicide bombers. So-called martyrs have been willing to kill themselves throughout the Middle East, Southeast Asia, and elsewhere on behalf of a number of causes and in the hope of killing as many of the enemy, variously defined, as possible. Few government officials and terrorism specialists anticipated this development, although there were some precursors.

Current worries about nuclear terrorism focus on Pakistan. The fact that the country is a nuclear power with a stockpile of such weapons and that it is the home, particularly in the FATA of jihadist groups presently staging terrorist attacks in both Pakistan and Afghanistan leads observers to put two and two together. The result of this calculation is a nuclear-armed terrorist group with few inhibitions about using these weapons. Will terrorism end then with a cataclysmic bang?

The answer is, probably not. Peter Bergen, the CNN terrorism analyst, thinks that claims by Osama bin Laden, Ayman al-Zawahiri, and company is largely bragging and boasting with few claims on reality. In the years following 9/11 these al-Qaeda leaders made public assertions about their access to nuclear weapons accompanied by blood-curdling threats against the West. These remarks, Bergen contends, were intended as propaganda or perhaps an exercise in self-delusion.[3] At best, these remarks might have been intended to induce the US and its allies to spend more money preparing for a virtually nonexistent threat.

Bergen points out that Iran has spent many years and billions of dollars in attempting to manufacture a nuclear weapon but has not as yet (by 2010) succeeded in this effort. If a state like Iran or any other malignant autocracy has struggled, it follows that manufacturing a nuclear weapon is well beyond the capacity of a networked terrorist organization. But what about stealing one?

The obvious contender is Pakistan. It is a nuclear power with an unstable national government and an abundant supply of terrorist groups as well as straightforward criminal organizations. So theft is a legitimate concern. But as Bergen and others point out, stealing a nuclear weapon is not so easy. It is not like robbing a bank or stealing a loaf of bread off the shelves of a grocery. For one thing these weapons are routinely equipped with fail-safe devices that prevent anyone without the appropriate codes from using them. For another, Pakistan's nuclear arsenal is evidently separated into its various components, with the core some distance from the other elements.

What about the possibility of a nuclear-armed state, e.g., North Korea, selling or offering a gift to a terrorist group such as al-Qaeda? Perhaps this is a possibility, but one that requires serious qualifications. Radio-active material or nuclear weapons are not all that easy to move from one place to another. Nations and international organizations monitor their movements. Another consideration: unlike terrorist groups, nations have names and addresses. If a nuclear weapon were to be used against a state by a terrorist group, the donor nation would be the target of retaliation by the target one. In other words, donating or selling a nuclear weapon to a terrorist group would likely prove self-destructive for the country involved and, as a consequence, is unlikely to occur.

The United States would likely be the first target of a nuclear attack in the event that a terrorist group possessed an atomic bomb. But again, as Bergen points out, none of the various plots, schemes, and cabals concocted by al-Qaeda or any other jihadist groups to attack the United States since 9/11 has involved a nuclear weapon. The one exception was a case involving Jose Padilla, a Hispanic-American al-Qaeda recruit. He was alleged to have plotted to set off a radiological weapon in New York City. But when Padilla's case went to trial the government dropped the charge; unintentional testimony to the fact that bragging and boasting can get a would-be terrorist into trouble.

How long does terrorism last? One way of responding to this question is by referring to David Rapoport and Dipak Gupta, authors mentioned earlier in this commentary (Chapters 1 and 2 respectively). We should recall Rapoport's observation that modern terrorism has come in four separable waves, based on dominant themes: anarchism, national independence, revolution, and religious beliefs. He notes that each of the first three waves crested and receded after about a generation, which he defined as a period of about thirty years.[4] Those who heard the call to action tend to lose their enthusiasm after reaching middle age. A younger generation of terrorist recruits may not share the same sense of commitment as their predecessors, but even if they do, the authorities may be better equipped to respond to the threat.

Is history likely to repeat itself with the fourth wave of modern terrorism? If it does, we should expect the decline of al-Qaeda and other Salafist jihadi groups in the not too distant future. We are now about a generation removed from the events that precipitated the formation of al-Qaeda and its extensive network of like-minded groups. Isn't it reasonable to believe this religiously driven apparatus will wither away like its long list of predecessors? Accordingly, some have suspected that al-Qaeda may be on its last legs or, to paraphrase Churchill, not its end, or beginning of its end but certainly the end of its beginning, that a combination of external pressure and internal fragmentation will cause its demise.[5]

Audrey Cronin wisely points out the dangers of historical determinism. The fact that terrorist groups have ended in particular ways in the past is no guarantee other groups will necessarily end the same way or combination of ways in the near future. Yet, Cronin writes: "By placing the logic of al-Qaeda's twenty-first-century strategy within the framework of how other campaigns have met their demise, the United States and its allies can construct an effective counter-strategy for ending al-Qaeda."[6] Such a strategy would be composed of the following five elements.

First, she argues in favor of demystifying al-Qaeda. Westerners should not use the name as an all-purpose term for everything that worries us about the Muslim world or even all violent groups opposed to Western values. Second, Cronin recommends exploiting already existing cleavages within the organization. Next, related to this recommendation, she suggest taking steps to "hive off" al-Qaeda's various constituent groups, groups with agendas of their own. Fourth, we should call attention to al-Qaeda's numerous mistakes and failures. Fifth and last, she thinks the US should encourage a backlash against al-Qaeda by its constituents or potential constituents.

The majority of these policies are already in place, put there typically by national governments most immediately concerned (e.g., Saudi Arabia and Indonesia) by the terrorist threat either on their own initiative or in conjunction with the United States and its allies. There are other components to an effective counter-al-Qaeda strategy that should be mentioned here. Defensive measures already put in place by the United States, other Western and Middle Eastern governments have already had a deterrent effect. For instance, intelligence operations have led to the arrest of many would-be terrorists over the last several years. Cutting off the sources of funding for al-Qaeda and related bands is also a high priority.

We should not forget the use of force. The terrorists certainly have not. Small groups with limited popular support operating locally have often been crushed or dismantled by police agencies. "Crushing" terrorist groups as a tactic does not appear particularly effective though with al-Qaeda and other transnational groups, particularly when they function within weak or failing states: Afghanistan, Yemen, and Somalia. There is another side to the story, however. In 2009 the Sri Lankan military was able to defeat the Tamil Tigers with the use of overwhelming force applied against its redoubt in the northern part of the country. What about "decapitation" or targeted killings? The terrorists themselves certainly believe in its effectiveness since they usually adopt this practice themselves and typically request its cessation when they enter negotiations with the authorities.

Studies of the impact of "decapitation" on terrorist groups have produced mixed results (see Chapter 2). At a minimum it seems fair to say that the arrest or apprehension of key figures in the groups has a stronger impact than simply killing them. The acquisition of intelligence, human and electronic, seems indispensable in this regard. On balance, we might conclude that "decapitation" provides a means for disrupting the terrorist group's operations that, in turn, provides the authorities with some breathing room. In the case of al-Qaeda, what will fill this space?

Not too long ago General David Petraeus, Commander of US forces in Afghanistan, remarked that the US cannot "kill its way to victory" in the case of al-Qaeda. Our response to this observation is two-fold. First, there is the matter of encouraging terrorists to turn away from violence. Saudi Arabia, Yemen, and Indonesia, among other affected nations, have undertaken rehabilitation programs directed at captured members of al-Qaeda and Jemaah Islamiah.[7] Participants in these programs hold discussions with Muslim scholars who stress the un-Islamic views of Osama bin Laden and his lieutenants. After some time elapses, deradicalized participants are then offered an opportunity for a return to normal lives.

Second, al-Qaeda's own internal dynamics may prove self-destructive. During the course of its existence, the organization and the various members of its network have killed far more Muslims than "infidels." This fact has made al-Qaeda increasingly unpopular in the Muslim world. In Algeria and Iraq, for example, al-Qaeda and the groups linked to it have murdered thousands of ordinary Muslims, often in the most barbaric ways imaginable. If al-Qaeda seeks to win the "hearts and minds" of the faithful, it seems to be losing the struggle.

Al-Qaeda also suffers from internal divisions, in part as the result of the above. For instance, Ayman Al-Zawahiri admonished leaders of AQI and the Armed Islamic Group in Algeria for killing many innocent Muslims for little reason, thereby alienating many members of the Umma (the community of believers) in a self-defeating manner. Related to this debate is the issue of the *takfir*: Who has the ability to declare an individual, a group of individuals, or a whole regime (e.g., Egypt and Saudi Arabia) to be apostates and thereby legitimate targets for attack? Al-Qaeda's leaders have concluded they possess this ability, but many Muslim clerics and members of the Muslim Brotherhood think otherwise.[8]

In addition there is conflict over tactics. If Israel, inside the House of Islam and in possession of Jerusalem, is the principal enemy, then why hasn't al-Qaeda done more to attack it? If the American presence in the Land of the Two Holy Sites is anathema, the equivalent of the Mongol conquest, than why hasn't al-Qaeda succeeded to achieving its expulsion?

At this point it is worth calling attention to the distinction between decay and destruction. There are some exceptions, but terrorist groups rarely end by agreeing to unconditional surrender, like Nazi Germany and Imperial Japan in 1945. More often they seem to decay until they dissolve or become insignificant. The end is more likely to be a whimper than a bang.

Another way of tackling the problem of how terrorist groups end is by following the work of Dipak Gupta and others in suggesting that terrorist "movements" have a natural history. They have a beginning, middle, and end.[9] Key to accelerating the "end" is findings ways of separating the terrorist group from its nominal constituents and followers. Rather than killing or decapitating the terrorist group's leaders, cutting off the head of the snake, the authorities would be more successful if they took steps to transform the group (and its ideas) into a pariah that is shunned by its potential supporters and recruits.

How long does this take? Some suggest that al-Qaeda and other Salafist jihadi groups are already on a downward trajectory (see pp. 34–35). In other words, the fourth wave of terrorism should be coming to an end in the not too distant future. Others contend that there are unusual elements to the current wave, i.e., the role of religion, which will serve to sustain it over a longer period of time than its predecessors. Dan Benjamin, Walter Laqueur, and others claim that "holy wars" and "crusades" don't end that fast.[10] The appropriate comparisons are not with the previous waves of modern terrorism but with the periods of intense religious excitement in both Islam and Christianity that endured over centuries. Religion has the capacity to arouse intense and long-lasting emotions that more mundane views of the world lack. The Red Brigades and Red Army Faction lasted for at best a few decades. The medieval Shiite group, the Assassins, pursued their murder campaign against Sunni leaders over a few centuries—until they were destroyed by Mongol invaders in the thirteenth century.

We should consider some alternative possibilities. One was proposed many years ago by the English anthropologist Colin Campbell when he referred to a "cultic milieu." In such a milieu particular groups with exotic religious understandings of the world, often apocalyptic, come and go. But the broad background conditions that gave rise to them remain virtually the same. Those belonging to this milieu share a rejection of secular values and normal religious practices. Instead they are drawn to esoteric beliefs about the way the world works and human destiny.[11]

Campbell intended his concept to apply to the array of small religious groups that appeared and continue to appear in the Western world in reaction to modern trends towards secularism with its corresponding loss of the magical elements in popular views about the way the world works. These days, both Japan and the United States abound with small religious groups committed to these quasi-magical views.

We might very apply the idea of the "cultic milieu" to al-Qaeda and other violent groups in the Muslim world. The jihad-based terrorist groups may be defeated in one way or another, while the milieu from which they have emerged remains intact. If Campbell's line of reasoning applies, we would predict the defeat of the current generation of Salafist jihadi groups to be followed by violent successor groups until the milieu that promotes their appearance shifts.

A second though related possibility is a revival. Terrorist groups long thought defeated are simply dormant. If not exactly in the same form and under the same name, terrorist groups reappear when "political entrepreneurs" believe the conditions are propitious. Old wine poured into different bottles. In Greece, for example, the anarchist and revolutionary group November 17 was eliminated by the police before the 2000 Olympic Games. Greece is presently suffering (2011) from severe economic problems that have sparked popular protests in Athens and elsewhere. New violent anarchist bands have appeared or reappeared to launch a new campaign of violence against the Greek state. In the United Kingdom, MI5 is now expressing concern about a renewal of terrorism in Northern Ireland because of dissatisfaction with the results of the peace agreement. In Italy a few years ago, a small group claiming to be the successors of the Red Brigades staged a series of train robberies on behalf of the revolution. In the United States a few years after the arrest and prosecution of members of the violent racial supremacist gang the Silent Brotherhood in 1984, a Silent Brotherhood II appeared in Boise, Idaho, which carried out a few anti-Semitic attacks before meeting the same fate as its predecessor.

In the context of the Middle Eastern struggle between Israel and the Palestinians, both Hamas and PIJ are still active, with the former ruling the Gaza Strip. At present (2011) both organizations have suspended their terrorist attacks, in an unofficial *hudna* or truce. Yet it would not take all that much for them to revive their terrorist attacks on Israeli civilians. And if they don't, there are likely new successor groups, funded by Iran or Syria, waiting to take their place. Terrorism is always a temptation for small groups of otherwise ineffectual extremists.

For political groups with a broader base of popular support, we should pay attention to what Charles Tilly, Sidney Tarrow, Doug McAdams, and other analysts of social movements describe as the "repertoire of contention."[12] These groups may expand their repertoire to include terrorism but, depending on the reaction to this means of expression, they may eliminate it from their repertoire as well—at least for a while. The career of Fatah is illustrative: from terrorism to party politics to terrorism (the al-Aqsa Martyrs' Brigades during the second Intifada) back to peaceful party politics.

Still another possible future for terrorism is a "fifth wave." If Rapoport's conception approximates reality and the current wave of religiously inspired terrorism is likely to wane in the not-too-distant future, what would be next? It does not seem all that likely that terrorism as a tactic will disappear, for reasons already discussed.

The cause or causes that might propel a "fifth wave" remain obscure, although neo-nationalism, some form of right-wing backlash against Third World immigrants, and disputes over the distribution and control of natural resources seem leading contenders. As far as terrorist tactics are concerned, the growing ability of the authorities to defeat stand-alone terrorist groups may produce the following.

First, we may be confronted by new types of "leaderless resistance."[13] Originally pioneered by anarchists at the end of the nineteenth century, the idea of "lone wolves" carrying out assassinations of prominent individuals as a means of sparking a mass revolution was updated two decades ago by the American Ku Klux Klan figure Louis Beam. In an Internet-distributed message, Beam argued that the FBI and other police authorities had come to infiltrate normally organized racist organizations. To avoid this trap, Beam advocated that single individuals or small autonomous cells take up the cause. Their only connections would be via the Internet and the mass media. These individuals would react to publicly available news developments by launching terrorist attacks on symbolic enemies of white power. Repeated often enough these killings would set off RAHOWA, or a racial holy war. The outcome of RAHOWA would be the restoration of white supremacy in the United States with dark-skinned people deported and Jews killed. The late neo-Nazi figure William Pierce wrote a novel, *Hunter*, showing how this goal could be accomplished.

While these ideas about RAHOWA remain in the realm of fantasy, Marc Sageman seeks to provide the concept with a strong dose of reality. He thinks that al-Qaeda is becoming or has already become a loosely linked network of small groups and single individuals that function without central direction. Thanks to the Internet these largely autonomous groups and individuals strike out at targets in the United States and the Western world as the possibilities arise. The Madrid commuter train bombings in 2004 would serve as a successful example.

In any case, those employing terrorist tactics during a "fifth wave" might come to rely on some version of "leaderless resistance" in the belief that the social media and new weapons technologies would make their job easier if not more successful.

They are by no means incompatible but a prospective "fifth wave" of terrorism may very well be part of a broader insurgency. Of course there is some danger of simply projecting the present (i.e., Afghanistan and Iraq) into the future. Yet it is difficult to ignore the fact that terrorism has been most successful in the past when it has been used in conjunction with other tactics (see Chapter 4).[14] This judgment though needs to be qualified.

Connable and Libicki review eighty-nine cases of insurgencies and reach the conclusion that: "Broad terror campaigns by insurgents correlate with insurgent defeat, but selective terror attacks that do not kill innocent civilians correlate with a marked insurgent advantage."[15] Insurgent success and mass casualty terrorism seem to flow in different directions, the more of the latter the less likely the former. What follows from this generalization?

During the present era of what many observers have characterized as the "new terrorism" the trend has been for terrorists to strike at targets on an indiscriminate basis. Bryan Jenkins' old observation that "terrorists want a lot of people watching, not a lot of people dead" has been overtaken by events. At least since the advent of the "fourth wave" of religious terrorism in the 1980s, the tendency has been towards greater lethality. Suicide bombings have become the signature form of attacks as terrorists in or from the Middle East and South Asia have sought to kill large numbers of people in the most gruesome ways imaginable. Potential "fifth wave" terrorist groups may very well confront a conundrum or a strategic choice. The use of indiscriminate killings may forecast their ultimate strategic defeat, alienating the public(s), and causing governments to intensify their counterterrorism efforts. On the other hand, if they think in tactical terms, mass killings seem to have certain advantages.

This type of blood-letting satisfies one of the basic needs of those who wage terrorist campaigns: revenge. In the immediate aftermath of the 9/11 attacks little statuettes were manufactured and sold in the Gaza Strip and other parts of the Middle East showing a plane crashing into a miniature skyscraper. In other places, crowds cheered as news of 9/11 spread. For some time Osama bin Laden was wildly popular throughout the region because of his dexterity in plotting the deaths of thousands. He managed to achieve revenge against the United States and the West that others only dreamed of.

At the same time, terrorist attacks that cause mass casualties have certain immediate tactical benefits. Among other things, they demonstrate the failure of governments to prevent them and in that sense weaken public support for those in power. They sometimes coerce governments into making concrete concessions to whatever immediate aims the terrorists seek (e.g., withdrawal of American forces from Lebanon).

These outcomes seem to leave new terrorists or potential "fifth wave" terrorists with a dilemma. They may be able to achieve tactical benefits but at the cost of strategic failure. In other words, the use of mass casualty attacks likely may be self-defeating. This is not to say, of course, these attacks may not be used for the foreseeable future.

Postscript

The killing of Osama bin Laden at the end of May 2011 by a US special forces unit (Seal Team 6) naturally raises important questions about the future of al-Qaeda. Does this decapitation mean that the organization itself will shortly dwindle into insignificance? Or, does it seem likely that al-Qaeda and its affiliates will absorb this blow and continue on as before?

Readers will hardly be astonished when I report that opinions on the matter are divided. Bruce Hoffman has asserted that decapitating the leaders of terrorist organizations has rarely produced the desired results. He notes that during the 1990s Israeli forces managed to kill a succession of Hamas leaders without stopping terrorist attacks on Israeli civilians. He also calls to our attention the fact that, in 2006, American forces managed to kill Abu Mus'ab Al-Zarqawi, the blood-thirsty leader of al-Qaeda in Iraq, without putting an end to his band, though Hoffman admits the killing did cause significant disruption.[1] He even points out that during the struggle for Algerian independence during the 1950s the French managed to capture virtually the entire FLN leadership without this blow seriously disrupting the cause.

In Chapter 2 we referred to the work of Jenna Jordan.[2] Her findings led to the conclusion that terrorist groups that were long-lasting and based on religious ideals seemed unaffected by the targeted killing of their leaders. So, if we assume the accuracy of her analysis, Jordan's results reinforce Hoffman's view that bin Laden's death will not lead to al-Qaeda's demise.

There is another side to the story, though. The context in which bin Laden was killed includes the Arab Spring and the mass protests in Tunisia, Egypt, Yemen, Bahrain, Libya, and Syria. The demands of the young protestors have rarely included the forceful imposition of the Sharia and the establishment of Taliban-style regimes throughout the region. As Peter Bergen and others have pointed out, the young people involved in these uprisings have demanded jobs, an end to arbitrary rule by despots, and the establishment of governments responsive to the will of the people.[3] And as Philip Mudd, another terrorism analyst puts it:

> With the death of Osama bin Laden . . . Americans will be safer in the long-term, without bin Laden's magnetic appeal al-Qaeda's revolutionary movement will likely wither and its message, combined with peaceful revolutions in the Arab world will lose credibility.[4]

However, the short term is a different matter, as al-Qaeda affiliates, in Yemen especially, seek to take advantage of the turmoil associated with the Arab Spring to stage new attacks in revenge for the death of bin Laden.

Notes

1 Introduction

1 By terrorism we mean "premeditated, politically motivated violence perpe-trated against noncombatant targets by sub-national groups or clandestine agents, usually intended to influence an audience" (Title 22, United States Code, Section 2656f (d)).

2 Jena McNeil, James Carafano, and Jessica Zuckerman, "30 Plots Foiled: How the System Worked," www.heritage.org/Research Reports/2010/04 (last accessed April 29, 2010); the pace of planned attacks may be increasing. Bruce Hoffman reports that there were nine such terrorist plots discovered during 2009: "American Jihad," *The National Interest* 107 (May/June 2010): 17–27.

3 See, for example, Abu Bakr Naji, *The Management of Savagery* trans. William McCants (West Point, NY: Combating Terrorism Center, 2006), http://ctc.usma. edu (last accessed May 23, 2006). Funding for this translation was provided by the John M. Olin Institute for Strategic Studies at Harvard University.

4 David Rapoport, "The Four Waves of Modern Terrorism," in Audrey Cronin and James Ludes (Eds.) *Attacking Terrorism* (Washington, DC: Georgetown University Press, 2004), pp. 46–73.

5 Paul Wilkinson, *Terrorism versus Democracy* (London: Routledge, 2006), p. 1.

6 See, for example, Brigitte Nacos, *Mass-Mediated Terrorism* (Lanham, MD: Rowman & Littlefield, 2002); Gabriel Weimann, *Terror on the Internet* (Washington, DC: USIP Press, 2006).

7 John Horgan, "Deradicalization or Disengagement?" *Perspectives on Terrorism* 2:4 (February 2008), pp. 3–14; Richard Barrett and Laila Bokhari, "De-radicalization and Rehabilitation Programs Targeting Religious Terrorists and Extremists in the Muslim World," in Tore Bjørgo and John Horgan (Eds.) *Leaving Terrorism Behind* (New York: Routledge, 2009), pp. 170–192.

8 Martha Crenshaw, "Pathways Out of Terrorism: A Conceptual Framework," in L. Sergio Germani and D.R. Kaarthikeyan (Eds.), *Pathways Out of Terrorism and Insurgency* (Elgin, IL: New Dawn Press, 2005), pp. 3–11.

9 On this topic see especially, Audrey Cronin, "How al Qaeda Ends," *International Security* 31:1 (2006): 7–48; Martha Crenshaw, "How Terrorism Declines," *Terrorism and Political Violence* 3:1 (1991): 69–87; Jeffrey Ross and Ted Gurr, "Why Terrorism Subsides," *Comparative Politics* 21(1989): 405–426.

10 See, for example, Leonard Weinberg, "The Red Brigades," in Robert Art and Louise Richardson (Eds.) *Democracy and Counterterrorism* (Washington, DC: USIP Press, 2007), pp. 25–62.

11 Lawrence Wright, *The Looming Tower* (New York: Alfred Knopf, 2006), p. 257.

12 Robin Erica Wagner-Pacifici, *The Moro Morality Play* (Chicago: University of Chicago Press, 1986), pp. 220–225.

13 Jeffrey Ross and Ted Gurr, "Why Terrorism Subsides," *Comparative Politics* 21 (1989): 405–426.

14 Omar Ashour, "De-radicalization of Jihad?" *Perspectives on Terrorism* 2:5 (2008): 11–14.

15 Cynthia Irvin, *Militant Nationalism* (Minneapolis, MN: University of Minnesota Press, 1999), p. 25.

16 Irvin, p. 28.

17 For a description see Walter Laqueur, *The Age of Terrorism* (Boston, MA: Little, Brown & Co., 1987), pp. 259–261.

18 Max Abrahams, "Why Terrorism Does Not Work," *International Security* 31:2 (Fall 2006): 42–78.

19 See Daniel Byman, *Deadly Connections* (New York: Cambridge University Press, 2005), pp. 155–185.

20 Leonard Weinberg and Ami Pedahzur, *Political Parties and Terrorist Groups* (New York: Routledge, 2003), pp. 61–85.

21 See, for example, Roger MacGinty and John Darby, *Guns and Government* (London: Palgrave, 2002), pp. 29–85.

22 Brian Crozier, *The Rebels* (Boston, MA: Beacon Press, 1960), pp. 255–267.

23 Walter Laqueur, *Guerrilla* (Boston, MA: Little, Brown & Co., 1976), p. 271.

2 The ends of the affair

1 Walter Laqueur, "Reflections on Terrorism," *Foreign Affairs* (Fall, 1986): 86–100.

2 David Rapoport, "Terrorism," in M. Hawkeworth and M. Kogan (Eds.) *Encyclopedia of Government and Politics* vol. 2 (London: Routledge, 1992), pp. 1061–1082.

3 Carlos Marighella, "From the 'Minimanual'" and Abraham Guillen, "Urban Guerilla Strategy," in Walter Laqueur (Ed.) *Voices of Terror* (New York: The Reed Press, 2004), pp. 370–383.

4 James Kohl and John Litt, *Urban Guerrilla Warfare in Latin America* (Cambridge, MA: MIT Press, 1974), p. 318.

5 Richard Gillespie, *Soldiers of Peron* (Oxford: Clarendon Press, 1982), pp. 47–88.

6 See, for example, Walter Laqueur, *Guerrilla* (Boston, MA: Little, Brown & Co., 1976), pp. 100–151.

7 Richard Gillespie, "Political Violence in Argentina," in Martha Crenshaw (Ed.) *Terrorism in Context* (University Park, PA: Pennsylvania State University Press, 1995), pp. 221–225.

8 See, for example, Anthony Joes, *Fascism in the Contemporary World* (Boulder, CO: Westview Press, 1978), pp. 157–164.

9 In the 1970s the Montoneros' support for Peron inspired a number of violent neo-fascist groups in Italy. Groups active in Rome like Third Position and

Without Truce sought to appeal to the far-left terrorist groups under the slogan "one enemy, one struggle." They saw in the Mononeros kindred spirits.

10 Gillespie, *Soldiers of Peron*, p. 145. The statement seems remarkably similar to one made by the Nazi figure Rudolph Hess about the *Führer* at a Nuremberg party rally.

11 See, for example, Roger Fontaine, "Argentina," in Yonah Alexander (Ed.) *Combating Terrorism* (Ann Arbor, MI: University of Michigan Press, 2002), pp. 62–83.

12 Alastair Horne, *A Savage War of Peace* (New York: New York Review Press, 2006), pp. 25–30.

13 Martha Crenshaw Hutchinson, *Revolutionary Terrorism* (Stanford, CA: Hoover Institution Press, 1978), pp. 12–14.

14 Martha Crenshaw, "The Effectiveness of Terrorism During the Algerian War," in Martha Crenshaw (Ed.) *Terrorism in Context* (University Park, PA: Pennsylvania University Press, 1995), pp. 485–494.

15 For a discussion see Stanley Hoffman, *Decline or Renewal? France Since the 1930s* (New York: The Viking Press, 1974), pp. 63–110.

16 Horne, pp. 218–219.

17 Brendan O'Leary, "The IRA: Looking Back; Mission Accomplished?" in Marianne Heiberg, Brendan O'Leary, and John Tirman (Eds.) *Terror Insurgency and the State* (Philadelphia, PA: University of Pennsylvania Press, 2007), pp. 189–202.

18 Tim Pat Coogan, *The IRA* (New York: Palgrave, 2002), pp. 3–37.

19 Tim Pat Coogan, *The Troubles* (London: Random House, 1996), pp. 70–95.

20 Coogan, *The Troubles*, p. 159.

21 Roger MacGinty and John Darby, *Guns and Government: The Management of the Northern Ireland Peace Process* (London: Palgrave, 2002), pp. 29–85.

22 Dipak Gupta, *Understanding Terrorism and Political Violence* (New York: Routledge, 2008), pp. 64–101.

23 Seth Jones and Martin Libicki, *How Terrorist Groups End* (Santa Monica, CA: The Rand Corporation, 2008), pp. 1–43.

24 See especially Audrey Cronin, *How Terrorism Ends* (Princeton, NJ: Princeton University Press, 2009), pp. 207–222.

25 For a discussion see Paul Wilkinson, *Terrorism versus Democracy*, 2nd ed. (London: Routledge, 2006), pp. 61–88.

26 See, for example, John Augustus Norton, *Hezbollah* (Princeton, NJ: Princeton University Press, 2007), pp. 71–112.

27 Jones and Libicki comment: "In generating these percentages, we excluded from the original 648 groups (1) that were still active (244 groups) and (2) those that ended because of splintering, since the members still used terrorism (136 groups)."

28 Cronin, pp. 208–209.

29 Christopher Hewitt, *The Effectiveness of Anti-Terrorism Policies* (Washington, DC: University Press of America, 1984), pp. 35–42.

30 In addition to *How Terrorism Ends* (see Note 24 above) these are "How al-Qaida Ends," *International Security* 31:1 (Summer 2006): 7–48; and *Ending Terrorism* Adelphi Paper 394 (London: Routledge, 2008).

31 Rumor has it that the *Normandy*, a luxury liner turned into a troop carrier, was deliberately capsized at dockside in New York as a way of demonstrating the disruptive power of the dockworkers' union.

32 For a discussion see Louise Richardson, *What Terrorists Want* (New York: Random House, 2006), pp. 72–103.

33 Lewis Feuer, *The Conflict of Generations* (New York: Basic Books, 1969), pp. 3–49.

34 Jessica Stern, *Terror in the Name of God* (New York: HarperCollins, 2003), pp. 189–190.

35 Alex Schmid and Albert Jongman, *Political Terrorism* (New Brunswick, NJ: Transaction, 1988), pp. 497–700; MIPT Terrorism Knowledge Base, www.tkb. org (last accessed December 10, 2010); Officer of the Coordinator of Counter-Terrorism, www.usis.usemb.se/terror (last accessed December 1, 2010). These sources provided us with information about the characteristics of 2,242 violent political groups formed during the twentieth century and the early years of the twenty-first. When important information about a certain group was missing, we used additional resources, especially government reports, court protocols, and reliable Internet sources. Once the information was collected it was encoded into a quantitative data set (using SPSS software), allowing us to search for patterns and trends in the data. Not all the groups included warranted the designation "terrorist group." We included groups only if they met the following criteria: 1) the group was described as either "terrorist" or "urban guerrilla"; 2) the group's activities included violent acts that were perpetrated to achieve some type of political aim; 3) the acts it committed were intended to achieve some psychological or symbolic effect; and 4) were carried out against noncombatants or civilians (Latin American "death squads" were included). Based on these standards we identified a total of 430 groups that warranted the label "terrorist group." For a more complete description of the data set see Leonard Weinberg, Ami Pedahzur, and Arie Perliger, *Political Parties and Terrorist Groups*, 2nd ed. (New York: Routledge, 2009), pp. 28–29.

36 Jenna Jordan, "When Heads Roll: The Effectiveness of Leadership Decapitation," *Security Studies* 18:4 (2009): 710–755; Austin Long, "Assessing the Success of Targeted Killing," *CTC Sentinel* 3:11–12 (November 2010): 19–21; Mohammed Hafez and Joseph Hatfield, "Do Targeted Killings Work?" *Studies in Conflict and Terrorism* 29 (2006): 359–382.

37 Alex Wilner, "Targeted Killings in Afghanistan," *Studies in Conflict and Terrorism* 33 (2010): 307–329; Edward Kaplan, Alex Mintz, Shaul Mishal, and Claudio Samban, "What Happened to Suicide Bombings in Israel?" *Studies in Conflict and Terrorism* 28 (2005): 225–235.

38 Wilner, p. 319.

39 See, for example, Max Abrahams, "Are Terrorists Really Rational?" *Orbis* 48:3 (2004): 533–549.

3 Defeat

1 Max Abrahams, "Why Terrorism Does Not Work," *International Security* 31:2 (Fall 2006): 42–78; John Mueller, *Overblown* (New York: The Free Press, 2006), pp. 13–28; Alan Dershowitz, *Why Terrorism Works* (New Haven, CT: Yale University Press, 2002).

2 See, for example, Lorenzo Vidino, *Al Qaeda in Europe* (Amherst, NY: Prometheus Books, 2006), pp. 291–335.

3 For a general discussion see Robert Pape, *Dying to Win* (New York: Random House, 2005), pp. 27–37.

4   See, for example, Stephen Hopgood, "Tamil Tigers, 1987–2002," in Diego Gambetta (Ed.) *Making Sense of Suicide Missions* (New York: Oxford University Press, 2005), pp. 43–76.

5   See, for example, *Besieged, Displaced, and Detained* (New York: Human Rights Watch, 2008).

6   Brendan O'Duffy, "LTTE: Majoritarianism, Self-Determination, and Military-to-Political Transition in Sri Lanka," in Marianne Heiberg, Brendan O'Leary, and John Tirman (Eds.) *Terror Insurgency and the State*. (Philadelphia, PA: University of Pennsylvania Press, 2007), p. 259.

7   O'Duffy, p. 259.

8   Mia Bloom, *Dying to Kill* (New York: Columbia University Press, 2005), pp. 50–51.

9   Thomas Marks, "Sri Lanka and the Liberation Tigers of Tamil Eelam," in Robert Art and Louise Richardson, *Democracy and Counterterrorism* (Washington, DC: USIP Press, 2007), p. 490.

10   Bloom, p. 54–55.

11   Martha Crenshaw, "Democracy, Commitment Problems and Ethnic Conflict," in David Rapoport and Leonard Weinberg (Eds.) *The Democratic Experience and Political Violence* (London: Frank Cass, 2010), pp. 135–159.

12   Robert Kaplan, "Buddha's Savage Peace," *The Atlantic* (September 2009): 56–61.

13   For a discussion see Guy Faure, "Deadlocks in Negotiation Dynamics," in William Zartman and Guy Faure (Eds.) *Escalation and Negotiations in International Conflicts* (New York: Cambridge University Press, 2005), pp. 23–52.

14   Franco Ferraresi, *Threats to Democracy* (Princeton, NJ: Princeton University Press, 1996), pp. 51–68.

15   Rossario Mina, "Il terrorismo di destra," in Donatella della Porta (Ed.) *Terrorismi in Italia* (Bologna: Il Mulino, 1984), pp. 21–72.

16   For a discussion see Alessandro Silj, *Never Again Without a Rifle* (New York: Karz Publishers, 1977), pp. 96–157.

17   Ferraresi, pp. 144–145.

18   Quoted in Ferraresi, p. 158.

19   David Moss, *The Politics of Left-Wing Violence in Italy, 1969–85* (New York: St. Martin's, 1989), pp. 76–80.

20   Robin Erica Wagner-Pacifici, *The Moro Morality Play* (Chicago: University of Chicago Press, 1986), pp. 22–61.

21   Vittorio Grevi, "La risposta legisaltiva al terrorismo," in Gianfranco Pasquino (Ed.) *La prova delle armi* (Bologna: Il Mulino, 1984), pp. 17–91.

22   Vali Nasr, *The Shia Revival* (New York: W.W. Norton, 2006), p. 238.

23   For a discussion see Said Amir Arjomand, *The Turban for the Crown* (New York: Oxford University Press, 1989), pp. 103–146.

24   See, for example, Sepehr Zabih, *Iran Since the Revolution* (Baltimore, MD: Johns Hopkins University Press, 1982), pp. 138–159.

25   Shaul Bakhash, *The Reign of the Ayatollahs* (New York: Basic Books, 1984), pp. 219–227.

26   Dilip Hiro, *Iran under the Ayatollahs* (London: Routledge, 1985), pp. 194–197.

27   Walter Laqueur, *The Age of Terrorism* (Boston, MA: Little, Brown & Co., 1987), p. 260.

28   Bakhash, p. 220.

29 John Stephan, *The Russian Fascists* (New York: Harper & Row, 1978), pp. 187–208.
30 For a discussion see Audrey Cronin, *How Terrorism Ends* (Princeton, NJ: Princeton University Press, 2009), pp. 14–34.
31 See, for example, Peter Bergen and Katherine Tiedemann, "The Year of the Drone," *Counterterrorism Strategy Initiative Policy Paper*, New America Foundation, February 24, 2010.
32 Jenna Jordan, "When Heads Roll: Assessing the Effectiveness of Leadership Decapitation," *Security Studies* 18:4: 719–755.
33 Petter Nesser, "Joining Jihadi Terrorist Cells in Europe," in Magnus Ranstorp (Ed.) *Understanding Violent Radicalization* (New York: Routledge, 2010), pp. 97–114.
34 Quoted in Gustavo Gorriti, *The Shining Path* (Chapel Hill, NC: University of North Carolina Press, 1999), pp. 57–58.
35 Scott Palmer, "The Revolutionary Terrorism of Peru's Shining Path," in Martha Crenshaw (Ed.) *Terrorism in Context* (University Station, PA: Pennsylvania University Press, 1995), p. 266.
36 David Scott Palmer, "Terror in the Name of Mao," in Robert Art and Louise Richardson (Eds.) *Democracy and Counterterrorism* (Washington, DC: USIP Press, 2007), p. 197.
37 Tina Rosenberg, *Children of Cain* (New York: Morrow, 1991), p. 153.
38 Daniel Metraux, *Aum Shinrikyo and Japanese Youth* (New York: University Press of America, 1999), pp. 1–7.
39 For his background and development see Robert Jay Lifton, *Destroying the World to Save It* (New York: Henry Holt, 1999), pp. 22–43.
40 Mark Juergensmeyer, *Terror in the Mind of God* (Berkeley, CA: University of California Press, 2001), pp. 102–116.
41 John Parachini and Katsuhisa Furukawa, "Japan and Aum Shinrikyo," in Robert Art and Louise Richardson (Eds.) *Democracy and Counterterrorism* (Washington, DC: USIP Press, 2007), pp. 531–562.
42 On the subject of student rebellion see Lewis Feuer, *The Conflict of Generations* (New York: Basic Books, 1969), pp. 385–435.
43 Dan Berger, *Outlaws of America* (Edinburgh, UK: AK Press, 2006), p. 26.
44 Jeremy Varon, *Bringing the War Home* (Berkeley, CA: University of California Press, 2004), pp. 74–112.
45 See, for example, Mathew Levitt, *Hamas* (New Haven, CT: Yale University Press, 2006), pp. 33–51.
46 Martha Crenshaw, "The Logic of Terrorism," in Walter Reich (Ed.) *Origins of Terrorism* (New York: Cambridge University Press, 1990), pp. 10–16.
47 Mohamed Hafez, "Tactics, *Takfir* and Anti-Muslim Violence," in Assaf Moghadam and Brian Fishman (Eds.) *Self-Inflicted Wounds* (West Point, NY: Combating Terrorism Center, 2010), pp. 19–44.
48 Anna Geifman, *Thou Shalt Kill: Revolutionary Terrorism in Russia, 1894–1917* (Princeton, NJ: Princeton University Press, 1993), pp. 84–122.
49 Tore Bjørgo and John Horgan (Eds.) *Leaving Terrorism Behind* (London: Routledge, 2009), pp. 17–65.
50 Cynthia Irvin, *Militant Nationalism* (Minneapolis, MT: University of Minnesota Press, 1999), p. 25.
51 Omar Ashour, "De-Radicalization of Jihad?" *Perspectives on Terrorism* II:5 (2008): 11–14.

52 Lisa Playdes and Lawrence Rubin, "Ideological Re-Orientation and Counter-Terrorism," *Terrorism and Political Violence* 20:8 (2008): 461–479.

4 Success

1 Alan Dershowitz, *Why Terrorism Works* (New Haven, CT: Yale University Press, 2002), pp. 36–88.
2 For a discussion of victory see William Martel, *Victory in War* (New York: Cambridge University Press, 2007), pp. 104–148.
3 Mathew Levitt, *Hamas* (New Haven, CT: Yale University Press, 2006), pp. 107–142.
4 For a discussion see Bard O'Neill, *Insurgency and Terrorism*, 2nd ed. (Washington, DC: Potomac Books, 2005), pp. 45–70.
5 Antonio de la Cova, *The Cuban Revolution*. www.latinamericanstudies.org/cuba-terrorism.htm (last accessed September 21, 2010).
6 US Army and US Marine Corps, *Counterinsurgency* FM 3-24/MCWP 3-33.5 (December 2006): 1–2.
7 O'Neill, p. 15.
8 Thomas Thornton, "Terror as a Weapon of Political Agitation," in Harry Eckstein (Ed.) *Internal War* (New York: The Free Press, 1964), pp. 92–95.
9 To capture this range of writing see Stathis Kalyvas, *The Logic of Violence in Civil War* (New York: Cambridge University Press, 2006), pp. 434–477.
10 Sidney Tarrow, *Power in Movement* (New York: Cambridge University Press, 1994), p. 23.
11 George Modelski, "International Settlement of Internal Wars," in James Rosenau (Ed.) *International Aspects of Civil Strife* (Princeton, NJ: Princeton University Press, 1964), pp. 122–153.
12 See, for example, William Zartman and Guy Faure, "The Dynamics of Escalation and Negotiations," in *Escalation and Negotiation in International Conflicts* (New York: Cambridge University Press, 2005), pp. 3–19.
13 Ben Connable and Martin Libicki, *How Insurgencies End* (Santa Monica, CA: The Rand Corporation, 2010).
14 See, for example, "State Repression and Enforcement Terrorism in Latin America," in Michael Stohl and George Lopez (Eds.) *The State as Terrorist* (Westport, CT: Greenwood, 1984), pp. 83–98.
15 Connable and Libicki, pp. 159–162.
16 Daniel Byman and Christine Fair, "The Case for Calling them Nitwits," *The Atlantic* (July/August 2010). www.theatlantic.com/magazine/archive/2010/07 (last accessed June 13, 2011).
17 See, for example, Robin Wright, *Sacred Rage* (New York: Simon & Schuster, 1985), pp. 69–110.
18 See, for example, Jillian Becker, *The PLO* (New York: St. Martin's, 1984), pp. 211–224.
19 See, for example, Vali Nasr, *The Shia Revival* (New York: W.W. Norton, 2007), pp. 84–85.
20 Thomas Friedman, *From Beirut to Jerusalem* (New York: Farrar, Strauss, Giroux, 1989), pp. 187–211.
21 Augustus Richard Norton, *Hezbollah* (Princeton, NJ: Princeton University Press, 2007), pp. 79–93.
22 Ami Pedahzur, *The Israeli Secret Services and the Struggle against Terrorism* (New York: Columbia University Press, 2009), pp. 85–87.

23 For a history of the war(s) see Stanley Karnow, *Vietnam: A History* (New York: Viking Press, 1983).

24 Karnow, p. 149.

25 Bernard Fall, *Street Without Joy* (Harrisburg, PA: The Stackpole Company, 1961), pp. 27–100.

26 Bernard Fall, *Hell in a Very Small Place* (New York: J.B. Lippincott, 1967), pp. 225–278.

27 "The Tiger and the Elephant: Viet Minh Strategy and Tactics," http://indochine54.free.fr/vm/tiger.html (last accessed March 21, 2011).

28 "The Tiger and the Elephant," p. 7.

29 For a discussion see David Kilcullen, *The Accidental Guerrilla* (New York: Oxford University Press, 2009), pp. 1–38.

30 Walter Laqueur, *Guerrilla* (Boston, MA: Little, Brown & Co., 1976), p. 271.

31 Jeffrey Race, *War Comes to Long An* (Berkeley, CA: University of California Press, 1972), p. 113.

32 Race, p. 135.

33 For an account see Michael Biggs, "Dying Without Killing: Self-Immolations, 1962–2002," in Diego Gambetta (Ed.) *Making Sense of Suicide Missions* (New York: Oxford University Press, 2005), pp. 173–2008.

34 These accounts were drawn from Thcavnam, which is available at: www.11thcavnam.co/education/namterror.htm (last accessed August 5, 2005).

35 Stephen Hosmer, *Viet Cong Repression and Its Implications for the Future* (Lexington, MA: Heath Lexington Books, 1970), pp. 55–56.

36 For an account see Douglas Pike, *The Viet Cong Strategy of Terror* (Washington, DC: Indochina Archive 1970), pp. 23–42.

37 V. Pohle, *The Viet Cong in Saigon: Tactics and Objectives During the Tet Offensive*, Rand Corporation, RM5799-ISA/ARPA: 8–22.

38 Don Oberdorfer, *TET!* (Baltimore, MD: The Johns Hopkins University Press, 2001), p. 142.

39 Laqueur, p. 287; Kalyvas, p. 169.

5 Transformation

1 For a discussion see Dipak Gupta, *Understanding Terrorism and Political Violence* (London: Routledge, 2008), pp. 146–160.

2 Jean Charles Brisard, *Zarqawi: The New Face of Al-Qaeda* (New York: Other Press, 2005), pp. 10–14.

3 Walter Laqueur, *The Age of Terrorism* (Boston, MA: Little, Brown & Co., 1987), pp. 17–18.

4 Paul Collier and Anke Hoeffler, "Greed and Grievance in Civil War," World Bank, CSAE WPS/2002-01.

5 Collier and Hoeffler, p. 1.

6 On the notion of "opportunity structure" readers should see Sidney Tarrow, *Power in Movement* (New York: Cambridge University Press, 1994), pp. 1–27.

7 James Fearon, "Why Do Some Civil Wars Last So Much Longer Than Others?" *Journal of Peace Research* 41:3 (May 2004): 275–301.

8 Jessica Stern, *Terror in the Name of God* (New York: Harper Collins, 2003), p. 189.

9 Colin Smith, *Carlos: Portrait of a Terrorist* (New York: Holt, Rinehart, 1976), *ad passim*.

10 For a general discussion see James Adams, *The Financing of Terror* (New York: Simon & Schuster, 1986), pp. 83–106.

11 For a discussion see Peter Waldmann, "Colombia and the FARC," in Robert Art and Louise Richardson (Eds.), *Democracy and Counterterrorism* (Washington, DC: USIP Press, 2007), pp. 221–260.

12 James Zackrison, "Colombia," in Yonah Alexander (Ed.) *Combating Terrorism* (Ann Arbor, MI: University of Michigan Press, 2002), pp. 116–159.

13 Stephanie Hanson, "FARC, ELN: Colombia's Left-Wing Guerrillas," Council of Foreign Relations (August 19, 2009), p. 3.

14 Angel Rabasa and Peter Chalk, *Colombian Labyrinth* (Santa Monica, CA: Rand Corporation, 2001), pp. 25–27.

15 See Alfredo Filler, "The Abu Sayyaf Group," *Terrorism and Political Violence* 14:4 (2002): 131–162.

16 Mark Bowden, "Jihadists in Paradise," *The Atlantic* (March 2007): 22–23.

17 Peter Chalk, Angel Rabasa, William Rosenau, and Leanne Piggott, *The Evolving Terrorist Threat to Southeast Asia* (Santa Monica, CA: Rand, 2009), pp. 51–52.

18 Bowden, p. 6.

19 Yossi Melman, *The Master Terrorist* (New York: Avon Books, 1986), pp. 49–64.

20 Patrick Seale, *Abu Nidal: A Gun for Hire* (London: Hutchinson, 1992), pp. 318–324.

21 Dan Byman, *Deadly Connections* (New York: Cambridge University Press, 2005), p. 38.

22 Seale, p. 49.

23 Gretchen Peters, *Crime and Insurgency in the Tribal Areas of Afghanistan and Pakistan* (West Point, NY: Combating Terrorism Center, 2010), pp. 11–13.

24 Peters, p. 24.

25 Peter Neumann, "The Bullet and the Ballot Box: The Case of the IRA," *Journal of Strategic Studies* 28:6 (2005): 941–975.

26 For a general discussion of the phenomenon see Leonard Weinberg and Ami Pedahzur, *Political Parties and Terrorist Groups* (New York: Routledge, 2003).

27 See, for example, Goldie Shabad and Francisco Jose Llera Ramo, "Political Violence in a Democratic State: Basque Terrorism in Spain," in Martha Crenshaw (Ed.) *Terrorism in Context* (University Park, PA: Pennsylvania State University Press, 1995), pp. 410–469.

28 Ami Pedahzur and Arie Perliger, *Jewish Terrorism in Israel* (New York: Columbia University Press, 2009), pp. 10–37.

29 J. Bowyer Bell, *Terror out of Zion* (New York: Avon Books, 1977), pp. 77–126.

30 For a description see Martin Gilbert, *Israel: A History* (New York: William Morrow, 1998), pp. 134–135.

31 Benny Morris, *Righteous Victims* (New York: Alfred Knopf, 1999), pp. 444–493.

32 See Neil Livingstone and David Halevy, *Inside the PLO* (New York: William Morrow, 1990), pp. 62–70.

33 Quoted in Yehoshafat Harkabi, "Al Fatah's Doctrine," in Walter Laqueur (Ed.) *Voices of Terror* (New York: Reed Press, 2004), p. 153.

34 William Quandt, Fuad Jabber, and Ann Mosely Lesch, *The Politics of Palestinian Nationalism* (Berkeley, CA: University of California Press, 1973), pp. 52–78.
35 Quoted in Ian Bickerton and Carla Klausner, *A History of the Arab–Israeli Conflict*, 6th ed. (New York: Prentice Hall, 2010), p. 173.
36 See Rashid Khalidi, *The Iron Cage* (Boston, MA: Beacon Press, 2006), pp. 156–157. The dialogue between the US and the PLO was interrupted because one of the factions under the "umbrella" staged a terrorist attack on the cruise ship Achille Lauro in the Mediterranean.
37 Barry Rubin, *The Transformation of Palestinian Politics* (Cambridge, MA: Harvard University Press, 1999), pp. 27–44.
38 Augustus Richard Norton, *Hezbollah* (Princeton, NJ: Princeton University Press, 2007), pp. 14–25.
39 Norton, p. 34.
40 Robin Wright, *Sacred Rage* (New York: Simon & Schuster, 1985), pp. 82–90.
41 Martin Kramer, "The Moral Logic of Hizbollah," in Walter Reich (Ed.) *Origins of Terrorism* (New York: Cambridge University Press, 1990), pp. 131–157.
42 Vali Nasr, *The Shia Revival* (New York: W.W. Norton, 2007), pp. 114–115.

6 Conclusions

1 "Obama: Nuclear Terrorism is the 'Single Biggest Threat' to US," *USA Today* (April 11, 2010): 1.
 2 See, for example, Graham Allison, *Nuclear Terrorism* (New York: Henry Holt, 2004), pp. 43–103.
 3 Peter Bergen, "Reevaluating Al-Qa'ida's Mass Destruction Capabilities," *CTC Sentinel* 3:9 (September 2010): 1–4.
 4 David Rapoport, "The Four Waves of Modern Terrorism," in Audrey Cronin and James Ludes (Eds.) *Attacking Terrorism* (Washington, DC: George Washington University Press, 2004), pp. 46–73.
 5 Audrey Cronin, *Ending Terrorism: Lessons for Defeating al-Qaeda* (London: Routledge, 2008), pp. 51–72.
 6 Cronin, p. 59.
 7 Jessica Stern, "Mind over Martyr," *Foreign Affairs* 89:1 (January/February 2010): 95–108.
 8 For detailed discussions of these fissures see Assaf Moghadam and Brian Fishman (Eds.) *Self-Inflicted Wounds: Debates and Discussions Within Al-Qaida and its Periphery* (West Point, NY: CTC, 2010).
 9 Dipak Gupta, *Understanding Terrorism and Political Violence* (New York: Routledge, 2008), pp. 82–101.
10 See, for example, Walter Laqueur, *No End to War* (New York: Continuum, 2003) and Dan Benjamin and Steven Simon, *The Next Attack* (New York: Henry Holt, 2005).
11 Colin Campbell, "The Cult, the Cultic Milieu and Secularization," in Jeffrey Kaplan and Helene Loow (Eds.), *The Cultic Milieu* (Walnut Creek, CA: Altamira Press, 2002), pp. 12–25.
12 See, for example, Sidney Tarrow, *The New Transnational Activism* (New York: Cambridge University Press, 2005), pp. 23–24.

13 See, especially, "Louis Beam," in Jeffrey Kaplan (Ed.) *Encyclopedia of White Power* (Walnut Creek, CA: Altamira Press, 2000), pp. 17–23; and Marc Sageman, *Leaderless Jihad* (Philadelphia, PA: University of Pennsylvania Press, 2008), pp. 125–178.
14 See also Ben Connable and Martin Libicki, *How Insurgencies End* (Santa Monica, CA: Rand Corporation, 2010), pp. xi–xviii.
15 Connable and Libicki, p. xvii.

Postscript

1 Bruce Hoffman, "Bin Ladin's Killing and its Effect on Al-Qa'ida: What Comes Next?" *CTC Sentinel* (May, 2011): 1–2.
2 Jenna Jordan, "When Heads Role: The Effectiveness of Leadership Decapitation," *Security Studies* 18 (2009): 710–755.
3 Peter Bergen, "Al Qaeda: the Loser in Arab Revolutions", available at: http://cnn.site.printhis (last accessed February 3, 2011).
4 Philip Mudd, "The Death of Usama bin Ladin," *CTC Sentinel* 4:6 (June 2011): 1.

Bibliography

Abrahams, Max (2004) "Are Terrorists Really Rational?" *Orbis* 48(3): 533–549.
Abrahams, Max (2006) "Why Terrorism Does Not Work," *International Security* 31(2): 42–78.
Adams, James (1986) *The Financing of Terror*. New York: Simon & Schuster.
Allison, Graham (2004) *Nuclear Terrorism*. New York: Henry Holt.
Arjomand, Said Amir (1989) *The Turban for the Crown*. New York: Oxford University Press.
Ashour, Omar (2008) "De-Radicalization of Jihad?" *Perspectives on Terrorism* II(5): 11–14.
Bakhash, Shaul (1984) *The Reign of the Ayatollahs*. New York: Basic Books.
Barrett, Richard and Laila Bokhari (2009) "De-radicalization and Rehabilitation Programs Targeting Religious Terrorists and Extremists in the Muslim World," in Tore Bjørgo and John Horgan (Eds.) *Leaving Terrorism Behind*. New York: Routledge, pp. 170–192.
Becker, Jillian (1984) *The PLO*. New York: St. Martin's, pp. 211–224.
Bell, J. Bowyer (1977) *Terror out of Zion*. New York: Avon Books.
Benjamin, Dan and Steven Simon (2005) *The Next Attack*. New York: Henry Holt.
Bergen, Peter (2010) "Reevaluating Al-Qa'ida's Mass Destruction Capabilities," *CTC Sentinel* 3(9): 1–4.
Bergen, Peter and Katherine Tiedemann (2010) "The Year of the Drone," *Counterterrorism Strategy Initiative Policy Paper*. New America Foundation, February 24.
Berger, Dan (2006) *Outlaws of America*. Edinburgh, UK: AK Press.
Bickerton, Ian and Carla Klausner (2010) *A History of the Arab–Israeli Conflict*, 6th ed. New York: Prentice Hall.
Biggs, Michael (2005) "Dying Without Killing: Self-Immolations, 1962–2002," in Diego Gambetta (Ed.) *Making Sense of Suicide Missions*. New York: Oxford University Press, pp. 173–2008.
Bjørgo, Tore and John Horgan (2009) *Leaving Terrorism Behind*. London: Routledge.
Bloom, Mia (2005) *Dying to Kill*. New York: Columbia University Press, pp. 50–51.
Bowden, Mark (2007) "Jihadists in Paradise," *The Atlantic* March: 22–23.

Brisard, Jean Charles (2005) *Zarqawi: The New Face of Al-Qaeda*. New York: Other Press.

Byman, Daniel (2005) *Deadly Connections*. New York: Cambridge University Press.

Byman, Daniel and Christine Fair "The Case for Calling them Nitwits," *The Atlantic* (July/August). www.theatlantic.com/magazine/archive/2010/07 (last accessed June 13, 2011).

Campbell, Colin (2002) "The Cult, the Cultic Milieu and Secularization," in Jeffrey Kaplan and Helene Loow (Eds.) *The Cultic Milieu*. Walnut Creek, CA: Altamira Press, pp. 12–25.

Chalk, Peter, Angel Rabasa, William Rosenau, and Leanne Piggott (2009) *The Evolving Terrorist Threat to Southeast Asia*. Santa Monica, CA: Rand.

Collier, Paul and Anke Hoeffler (2002) "Greed and Grievance in Civil War," World Bank. CSAE WPS/2002-01.

Connable, Ben and Martin Libicki (2010) *How Insurgencies End*. Santa Monica, CA: Rand Corporation.

Coogan, Tim Pat (1996) *The Troubles*. London: Random House.

Coogan, Tim Pat (2002) *The IRA*. New York: Palgrave.

Crenshaw Hutchinson, Martha (1978) *Revolutionary Terrorism*. Stanford, CA: Hoover Institution Press.

Crenshaw, Martha (1990) "The Logic of Terrorism," in Walter Reich (Ed.) *Origins of Terrorism*. New York: Cambridge University Press, pp. 10–16.

Crenshaw, Martha (1991) "How Terrorism Declines," *Terrorism and Political Violence* 3(1): 69–87.

Crenshaw, Martha (1995) "The Effectiveness of Terrorism During the Algerian War," in Martha Crenshaw (Ed.) *Terrorism in Context*. University Park, PA: Pennsylvania University Press, pp. 485–494.

Crenshaw, Martha (2005) "Pathways Out of Terrorism: A Conceptual Framework," in L. Sergio Germani and D.R. Kaarthikeyan (Eds.) *Pathways out of Terrorism and Insurgency*. Elgin, IL: New Dawn Press, pp. 3–11.

Crenshaw, Martha (2010) "Democracy, Commitment Problems and Ethnic Conflict," in David Rapoport and Leonard Weinberg (Eds.) *The Democratic Experience and Political Violence*. London: Frank Cass, pp. 135–159.

Cronin, Audrey (2006) "How al-Qaida Ends," *International Security* 31(1): 7–48.

Cronin, Audrey (2008) *Ending Terrorism: Lessons for Defeating al-Qaeda*. London: Routledge.

Cronin, Audrey (2009) *How Terrorism Ends*. Princeton, NJ: Princeton University Press.

Crozier, Brian (1960) *The Rebels*. Boston, MA: Beacon Press.

de la Cova, Antonio (2010) *The Cuban Revolution*. www.latinamericanstudies.org/cuba-terrorism.htm (last accessed September 21, 2010).

Dershowitz, Alan (2002) *Why Terrorism Works*. New Haven, CT: Yale University Press.

Fall, Bernard (1961) *Street Without Joy*. Harrisburg, PA: The Stackpole Company.

Fall, Bernard (1967) *Hell in a Very Small Place*. New York: J.B. Lippincott.

Faure, Guy (2005) "Deadlocks in Negotiation Dynamics," in William Zartman and Guy Faure (Eds.) *Escalation and Negotiations in International Conflicts*. New York: Cambridge University Press, pp. 23–52.

Fearon, James (2004) "Why Do Some Civil Wars Last So Much Longer Than Others," *Journal of Peace Research* 41(3): 275–301.

Ferraresi, Franco (1996) *Threats to Democracy*. Princeton, NJ: Princeton University Press.

Feuer, Lewis (1969) *The Conflict of Generations*. New York: Basic Books.

Filler, Alfredo (2002) "The Abu Sayyaf Group," *Terrorism and Political Violence* 14(4): 131–162.

Fontaine, Roger (2002) "Argentina," in Yonah Alexander (Ed.) *Combating Terrorism*. Ann Arbor, MI: University of Michigan Press, pp. 62–83.

Friedman, Thomas (1989) *From Beirut to Jerusalem*. New York: Farrar, Strauss, Giroux.

Geifman, Anna (1993) *Thou Shalt Kill: Revolutionary Terrorism in Russia, 1894–1917*. Princeton, NJ: Princeton University Press.

Gilbert, Martin (1998) *Israel: A History*. New York: William Morrow.

Gillespie, Richard (1982) *Soldiers of Peron*. Oxford: Clarendon Press.

Gillespie, Richard (1995) "Political Violence in Argentina," in Martha Crenshaw (Ed.) *Terrorism in Context*. University Park, PA: Pennsylvania State University Press, pp. 221–225.

Gorriti, Gustavo (1999) *The Shining Path*. Chapel Hill, NC: University of North Carolina Press.

Grevi, Vittorio (1984) "La risposta legisaltiva al terrorismo," in Gianfranco Pasquino (Ed.) *La prova delle armi*. Bologna: Il Mulino, pp. 17–91.

Guillen, Abraham (2004) "Urban Guerilla Strategy," in Walter Laqueur (Ed.) *Voices of Terror*. New York: The Reed Press.

Gupta, Dipak (2008) *Understanding Terrorism and Political Violence*. London: Routledge.

Hafez, Mohamed (2010) "Tactics, *Takfir* and Anti-Muslim Violence," in Assaf Moghadam and Brian Fishman (Eds.) *Self-Inflicted Wounds*. West Point, NY: Combating Terrorism Center, pp. 19–44.

Hafez, Mohammed and Joseph Hatfield (2006) "Do Targeted Killings Work?" *Studies in Conflict and Terrorism* 29: 359–382.

Hanson, Stephanie (2009) "FARC, ELN: Colombia's Left-Wing Guerrillas," Council of Foreign Relations. August 19: 3.

Harkabi, Yehoshafat (2004) "Al Fatah's Doctrine," in Walter Laqueur (Ed.) *Voices of Terror*. New York: Reed Press, p. 153.

Hewitt, Christopher (1984) *The Effectiveness of Anti-Terrorism Policies*. Washington, DC: University Press of America.

Hiro, Dilip (1985) *Iran Under the Ayatollahs*. London: Routledge.

Hoffman, Bruce (2010) "American Jihad," *The National Interest* 107: 17–27.

Hoffman, Stanley (1974) *Decline or Renewal? France since the 1930s*. New York: The Viking Press.

Hopgood, Stephen (2005) "Tamil Tigers, 1987–2002," in Diego Gambetta (Ed.) *Making Sense of Suicide Missions*. New York: Oxford University Press, pp. 43–76.

Horgan, John (2008) "Deradicalization or Disengagement?" *Perspectives on Terrorism* 2(4): 3–14.

Horne, Alastair (2006) *A Savage War of Peace*. New York: New York Review Press.

Human Rights Watch (2008) *Besieged, Displaced, and Detained*. New York: Human Rights Watch.

Irvin, Cynthia (1999) *Militant Nationalism*. Minneapolis, MN: University of Minnesota Press.

Jackson, David (2010) "Obama: Nuclear Terrorism is the 'Single Biggest Threat' to US," *USA Today*. April 11.

Joes, Anthony (1978) *Fascism in the Contemporary World*. Boulder, CO: Westview Press.

Jones, Seth and Martin Libicki (2008) *How Terrorist Groups End*. Santa Monica, CA: The Rand Corporation.

Jordan, Jenna (2009) "When Heads Roll: The Effectiveness of Leadership Decapitation," *Security Studies* 18(4): 710–755.

Juergensmeyer, Mark (2001) *Terror in the Mind of God*. Berkeley, CA: University of California Press, pp. 102–116.

Kalyvas, Stathis (2006) *The Logic of Violence in Civil War*. New York: Cambridge University Press.

Kaplan, Edward, Alex Mintz, Shaul Mishal, and Claudio Samban (2005) "What Happened to Suicide Bombings in Israel?" *Studies in Conflict and Terrorism* 28: 225–235.

Kaplan, Jeffrey (2000) *Encyclopedia of White Power*. Walnut Creek, CA: Altamira Press.

Kaplan, Robert (2009) "Buddha's Savage Peace," *The Atlantic* September: 56–61.

Karnow, Stanley (1983) *Vietnam: A History*. New York: Viking Press.

Khalidi, Rashid (2006) *The Iron Cage*. Boston, MA: Beacon Press.

Kilcullen, David (2009) *The Accidental Guerrilla*. New York: Oxford University Press.

Kohl, James and John Litt (1974) *Urban Guerrilla Warfare in Latin America*. Cambridge, MA: MIT Press.

Kramer, Martin (1990) "The Moral Logic of Hizbollah," in Walter Reich (Ed.) *Origins of Terrorism*. New York: Cambridge University Press, pp. 131–157.

Laqueur, Walter (1976) *Guerrilla*. Boston, MA: Little, Brown & Co.

Laqueur, Walter (1986) "Reflections on Terrorism," *Foreign Affairs* Fall: 86–100.

Laqueur, Walter (1987) *The Age of Terrorism*. Boston, MA: Little, Brown & Co.

Laqueur, Walter (2003) *No End to War*. New York: Continuum.

Levitt, Mathew (2006) *Hamas*. New Haven, CT: Yale University Press.

Lifton, Robert Jay (1999) *Destroying the World to Save It*. New York: Henry Holt.

Livingstone, Neil and David Halevy (1990) *Inside the PLO*. New York: William Morrow.

Long, Austin (2010) "Assessing the Success of Targeted Killing," *CTC Sentinel* 3(11–12): 19–21.

MacGinty, Roger and John Darby (2002) *Guns and Government: The Management of the Northern Ireland Peace Process*. London: Palgrave.

Marighella, Carlos (2004) "From the 'Minimanual'," in Walter Laqueur (Ed.) *Voices of Terror*. New York: The Reed Press.

Marks, Thomas (2007) "Sri Lanka and the Liberation Tigers of Tamil Eelam," in Robert Art and Louise Richardson (Eds.) *Democracy and Counterterrorism*. Washington, DC: USIP Press, p. 490.

Martel, William (2007) *Victory in War*. New York: Cambridge University Press.

McNeil, Jena, James Carafano, and Jessica Zuckerman (2010) "30 Plots Foiled: How the System Worked," *Backgrounder No. 2405*. The Heritage Foundation.

Melman, Yossi (1986) *The Master Terrorist*. New York: Avon Books.

Metraux, Daniel (1999) *Aum Shinrikyo and Japanese Youth*. New York: University Press of America.

Mina, Rossario (1984) "Il terrorismo di destra," in Donatella della Porta (Ed.) *Terrorismi in Italia*. Bologna: Il Mulino, pp. 21–72.

Modelski, George (1964) "International Settlement of Internal Wars," in James Rosenau (Ed.) *International Aspects of Civil Strife*. Princeton, NJ: Princeton University Press, pp. 122–153.

Moghadam, Assaf and Brian Fishman (2010) *Self-Inflicted Wounds: Debates and Discussions within Al-Qaida and its Periphery*. West Point, NY: CTC.

Morris, Benny (1999) *Righteous Victims*. New York: Alfred Knopf.

Moss, David (1989) *The Politics of Left-Wing Violence in Italy, 1969–85*. New York: St. Martin's.

Mueller, John (2006) *Overblown*. New York: The Free Press.

Nacos, Brigitte Lebens (2002) *Mass-Mediated Terrorism*. Lanham, MD: Rowman & Littlefield.

Naji, Abu Bakr (2006) *The Management of Savagery* trans. William McCants. West Point, NY: Combating Terrorism Center.

Nasr, Vali (2006) *The Shia Revival*. New York: W.W. Norton.

Nesser, Petter (2010) "Joining Jihadi Terrorist Cells in Europe," in Magnus Ranstorp (Ed.) *Understanding Violent Radicalization*. New York: Routledge, pp. 97–114.

Neumann, Peter (2005) "The Bullet and the Ballot Box: The Case of the IRA," *Journal of Strategic Studies* 28(6): 941–975.

Norton, Augustus Richard (2007) *Hezbollah*. Princeton, NJ: Princeton University Press.

O'Duffy, Brendan "LTTE: Majoritarianism, Self-Determination, and Military-to-Political Transition in Sri Lanka," in Marianne Heiberg, Brendan O'Leary, and John Tirman (Eds.) *Terror Insurgency and the State*. Philadelphia, PA: University of Pennsylvania Press, p. 259.

O'Leary, Brendan (2007) "The IRA: Looking Back; Mission Accomplished?" in Marianne Heiberg, Brendan O'Leary, and John Tirman (Eds.) *Terror Insurgency and the State*. Philadelphia, PA: University of Pennsylvania Press, pp. 189–202.

O'Neill, Bard (2005) *Insurgency and Terrorism*, 2nd ed. Washington, DC: Potomac Books.

Pape, Robert (2005) *Dying to Win*. New York: Random House.

Palmer, David Scott (1995) "The Revolutionary Terrorism of Peru's Shining Path," in Martha Crenshaw (Ed.) *Terrorism in Context*. University Station, PA: Pennsylvania University Press, p. 266.

Palmer, David Scott (2007) "Terror in the Name of Mao," in Robert Art and Louise Richardson (Eds.) *Democracy and Counterterrorism*. Washington, DC: USIP Press, p. 197.

Parachini, John and Katsuhisa Furukawa (2007) "Japan and Aum Shinrikyo," in Robert Art and Louise Richardson (Eds.) *Democracy and Counterterrorism*. Washington, DC: USIP Press, pp. 531–562.

Pedahzur, Ami (2009) *The Israeli Secret Services and the Struggle against Terrorism*. New York: Columbia University Press.

Pedahzur, Ami and Arie Perliger (2009) *Jewish Terrorism in Israel*. New York: Columbia University Press.

Peters, Gretchen (2010) *Crime and Insurgency in the Tribal Areas of Afghanistan and Pakistan*. West Point, NY: Combating Terrorism Center.

Playdes, Lisa and Lawrence Rubin (2008) "Ideological Re-Orientation and Counter-Terrorism," *Terrorism and Political Violence* 20(8): 461–479.

Quandt, William, Fuad Jabber, and Ann Mosely Lesch (1973) *The Politics of Palestinian Nationalism*. Berkeley, CA: University of California Press, pp. 52–78.

Rabasa, Angel and Peter Chalk (2001) *Colombian Labyrinth*. Santa Monica, CA: Rand Corporation.

Race, Jeffrey (1972) *War Comes to Long An*. Berkeley, CA: University of California Press.

Rapoport, David (1992) "Terrorism," in M. Hawkeworth and M. Kogan (Eds.) *Encyclopedia of Government and Politics*. London: Routledge, vol. 2, pp. 1061–1082.

Rapoport, David (2004) "The Four Waves of Modern Terrorism," in Audrey Cronin and James Ludes (Eds.) *Attacking Terrorism*. Washington, DC: Georgetown University Press, pp. 46–73.

Richardson, Louise (2006) *What Terrorists Want*. New York: Random House.

Rosenberg, Tina (1991) *Children of Cain*. New York: Morrow.

Ross, Jeffrey and Ted Gurr (1989) "Why Terrorism Subsides," *Comparative Politics* 21: 405–426.

Rubin, Barry (1999) *The Transformation of Palestinian Politics*. Cambridge, MA: Harvard University Press.

Sageman, Marc (2008) *Leaderless Jihad*. Philadelphia, PA: University of Pennsylvania Press.

Schmid, Alex and Albert Jongman (1988) *Political Terrorism*. New Brunswick, NJ: Transaction.

Seale, Patrick (1992) *Abu Nidal: A Gun for Hire*. London: Hutchinson.

Shabad, Goldie and Francisco Jose Llera Ramo (1995) "Political Violence in a Democratic State: Basque Terrorism in Spain," in Martha Crenshaw (Ed.) *Terrorism in Context* (University Park, PA: Pennsylvania State University Press), pp. 410–469.

Silj, Alessandro (1977) *Never Again Without a Rifle*. New York: Karz Publishers, pp. 96–157.

Sloan, John W. (1984) "State Repression and Enforcement Terrorism in Latin America," in Michael Stohl and George Lopez (Eds.) *The State as Terrorist*. Westport, CT: Greenwood, pp. 83–98.

Smith, Colin (1976) *Carlos: Portrait of a Terrorist*. New York: Holt, Rinehart.

Stephan, John (1978) *The Russian Fascists*. New York: Harper & Row.

Stern, Jessica (2003) *Terror in the Name of God*. New York: HarperCollins.

Stern, Jessica (2010) "Mind Over Martyr," *Foreign Affairs* 89(1): 95–108.

Tarrow, Sidney (1994) *Power in Movement*. New York: Cambridge University Press.

Tarrow, Sidney (2005) *The New Transnational Activism*. New York: Cambridge University Press.

"The Tiger and the Elephant: Viet Minh Strategy and Tactics." http://indochine54. free.fr/vm/tiger.html (last accessed March 21, 2011).

Thornton, Thomas (1964) "Terror as a Weapon of Political Agitation," in Harry Eckstein (Ed.) *Internal War*. New York: The Free Press, pp. 92–95.

US Army and US Marine Corps (2006) *Counterinsurgency*. FM 3-24/MCWP 3-33.5 December: 1–2.

Varon, Jeremy (2004) *Bringing the War Home*. Berkeley, CA: University of California Press.

Vidino, Lorenzo (2006) *Al Qaeda in Europe*. Amherst, NY: Prometheus Books.

Wagner-Pacifici, Robin Erica (1986) *The Moro Morality Play*. Chicago: University of Chicago Press.

Waldman, Pater (2007) "Colombia and the FARC," in Robert Art and Louise Richardson (Eds.) *Democracy and Counterterrorism*. Washington, DC: USIP Press, pp. 221–260.

Weimann, Gabriel (2006) *Terror on the Internet*. Washington, DC: USIP Press.

Weinberg, Leonard (2007) "The Red Brigades," in Robert Art and Louise Richardson (Eds.) *Democracy and Counterterrorism*. Washington, DC: USIP Press, pp. 25–62.

Weinberg, Leonard and Ami Pedahzur (2003) *Political Parties and Terrorist Groups*. New York: Routledge.

Weinberg, Leonard, Ami Pedahzur, and Arie Perliger (2009) *Political Parties and Terrorist Groups*, 2nd ed. New York: Routledge.

Wilkinson, Paul (2006) *Terrorism versus Democracy*, 2nd ed. London: Routledge.

Wilner, Alex (2010) "Targeted Killings in Afghanistan," *Studies in Conflict and Terrorism* 33: 307–329.

Wright, Lawrence (2006) *The Looming Tower*. New York: Alfred Knopf.

Wright, Robin (1985) *Sacred Rage*. New York: Simon & Schuster.

Zabih, Sepehr (1982) *Iran Since the Revolution*. Baltimore, MD: Johns Hopkins University Press.

Zackrison, James (2002) "Colombia," in Yonah Alexander (Ed.) *Combating Terrorism*. Ann Arbor, MI: University of Michigan Press, pp. 116–159.

Zartman, William and Guy Faure (2005) "The Dynamics of Escalation and Negotiations," in William Zartman and Guy Faure (Eds.) *Escalation and Negotiation in International Conflicts*. New York: Cambridge University Press, pp. 3–19.

Index